T0100237

Build Mobile Apps with SwiftUI and Firebase

Learn SwiftUI and Firebase by Building Real-World Applications Communicating with a Backend

Sullivan De Carli

Apress®

Build Mobile Apps with SwiftUI and Firebase: Learn SwiftUI and Firebase by Building Real-World Applications Communicating with a Backend

Sullivan De Carli
Charleville-Mézières, France

ISBN-13 (pbk): 978-1-4842-9283-9 ISBN-13 (electronic): 978-1-4842-9452-9
https://doi.org/10.1007/978-1-4842-9452-9

Managing Director, Apress Media LLC: Welmoed Spahr
Acquisitions Editor: Susan McDermott
Development Editor: James Markham
Coordinating Editor: Jessica Vakili

Distributed to the book trade worldwide by Springer Science+Business Media New York, 233 Spring Street, 6th Floor, New York, NY 10013. Phone 1-800-SPRINGER, fax (201) 348-4505, e-mail orders-ny@springer-sbm.com, or visit www.springeronline.com. Apress Media, LLC is a California LLC and the sole member (owner) is Springer Science + Business Media Finance Inc (SSBM Finance Inc). SSBM Finance Inc is a **Delaware** corporation.

For information on translations, please e-mail booktranslations@springernature.com; for reprint, paperback, or audio rights, please e-mail bookpermissions@springernature.com.

Apress titles may be purchased in bulk for academic, corporate, or promotional use. eBook versions and licenses are also available for most titles. For more information, reference our Print and eBook Bulk Sales web page at http://www.apress.com/bulk-sales.

Any source code or other supplementary material referenced by the author in this book is available to readers on the Github repository: https://github.com/Apress/Build-Mobile-Apps-with-SwiftUI-and-Firebase. For more detailed information, please visit http://www.apress.com/source-code.

Printed on acid-free paper

I'd like to thank Tiago, Luis, and all the people who helped me learn how to code along the way. I'd also like to thank my girlfriend and my family for their support.

Table of Contents

About the Author ix

About the Technical Reviewer xi

Chapter 1: Introduction to SwiftUI 1

Xcode Walk-Through 1

What Makes SwiftUI Different 8

Coding with SwiftUI 11

Summary 15

Chapter 2: Introduction to Firebase 17

What Is Firebase? 17

Setting Up a Firebase Account and Project 20

Firebase Walk-Through 24

Connect Your iOS Application to Firebase 27

You Might Be Wondering What This File Is For 34

Summary 41

Chapter 3: Playing with Firestore 43

Introducing the MVVM Design Pattern 44

Create Data to Firestore 46

Read Data from Firestore 55

Pass Data from Views 58

Update Data from Firestore..62

Delete Data from Firestore...65

Summary..68

Chapter 4: Authenticate Users with Firebase Auth............................71

Setting Up Firebase Authenticate...72

Manage User Sessions..75

Sign Up with Email and Password 79

What If You Forget Your Password? 85

Secure the Firestore Database..88

Security Rules 92

Summary..94

Chapter 5: Advanced Firestore 95

Introducing Our New Project...95

Why Are We Creating a New Firebase Project? 97

Call the Backend with Async/Await...100

Summary..104

Chapter 6: Manage Pictures with Firebase Storage 105

Access the iPhone Camera and Library 105

Upload Pictures to Firebase Storage..108

Integrate Large Documents with Firestore 112

Summary..116

Chapter 7: Authenticate with Apple..117

Set Up the Project and "Sign in with Apple" 118

Integrate "Sign in with Apple"...120

Summary..128

Chapter 8: Adding Features Without Coding 129

Exploring Firebase Extension 129

Track Our App Usage with Analytics 132

Securing Our Database 134

Summary 135

Correction to: Build Mobile Apps with SwiftUI and Firebase C1

Index 137

About the Author

Sullivan De Carli is currently Consultant for Deloitte, where he works as an iOS developer with several Fortune 500 companies as clients. He began his development journey in 2017 and graduated from the Apple Developer Academy in Naples, Italy, in 2020. He has built apps for personal projects and successful entrepreneurial ventures.

About the Technical Reviewer

Alexander Nnakwue is a self-taught software engineer with experience in backend and full-stack engineering. With an experience spanning more than four years, he loves to solve problems at scale. Currently, he is interested in startups, open source web development, and distributed systems. In his spare time, he loves watching soccer and listening to all genres of music.

The original version of this book was revised. A correction to this book is available at https://doi.org/10.1007/978-1-4842-9452-9_9

CHAPTER 1

Introduction to SwiftUI

This first chapter is meant for beginners in iOS development. I will walk you through the main functionalities of Xcode, your tool to create projects and run code. Then, we will create a simple application: a map displaying a few places.

This way, we will explore some SwiftUI APIs to build the user interface and some basics of Swift such as creating a model. Let's get started!

Xcode Walk-Through

To build an iOS application, you first need Xcode. This software made by Apple will be your program to write Swift code, create a user interface, build and debug your project, and much more. Think of it like Photoshop for photography or Sketch and Figma for UI design.

The software is available on the Mac App Store; you can easily download it from there. Navigate to the App Store on your Mac and search for Xcode, and then click DOWNLOAD (I have "OPEN" since I already downloaded it):

© Sullivan De Carli 2023, corrected publication 2023
S. De Carli, *Build Mobile Apps with SwiftUI and Firebase*,
https://doi.org/10.1007/978-1-4842-9452-9_1

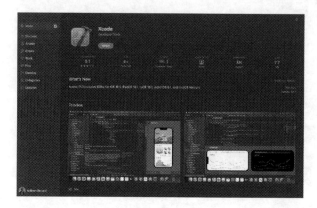

Figure 1-1. *Download Xcode from the App Store*

At the time of writing, the latest version is Xcode 14.1. I recommend you download at least Xcode 14; otherwise, a lot of functionalities will not be replicable throughout the book.

The download will take some time since it is quite a heavy program (7GB). Once you have downloaded it, you can open it. It will ask you if you want to download additional components for macOS and watchOS. You can skip this step since we only need iOS for the scope of this book.

Then, this page will appear, inviting you to start a project:

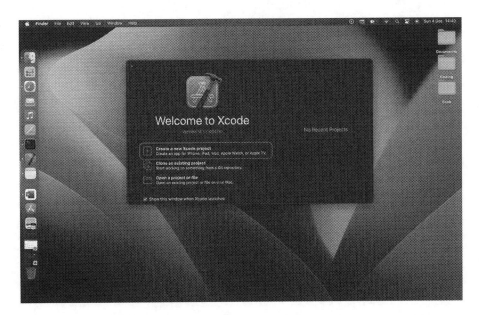

Figure 1-2. *Xcode welcome screen*

Click Create a new Xcode project, and the following page will appear:

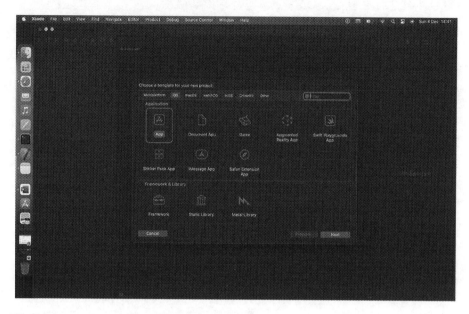

Figure 1-3. *Xcode – choosing a template*

Xcode will suggest to you a series of templates. In fact, you can build a lot of things using the Swift language such as an Apple Watch app, a game that runs on the iPhone, a Safari extension, or a utility app for Mac. We will select *App* from the iOS platform for now. It will be the same for the other projects although our application will also be able to run on the iPad.

Now, I invite you to enter the word **Discover**; this is going to be the name of our first project written with SwiftUI.

Also, make sure that the SwiftUI framework is selected together with the Swift language.

(Make sure to have your name or enterprise in the Team field. If you're new to Xcode, it is your Apple account that you use for the App Store. That should be your team's name. For me it is "Sullivan De Carli (Personal Team)."

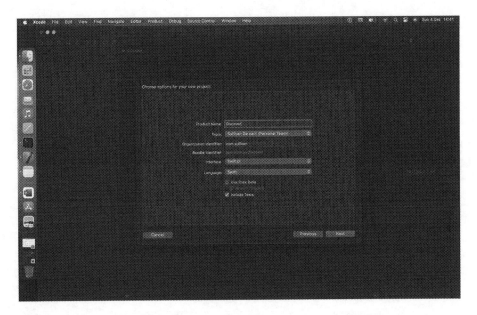

Figure 1-4. *Xcode – settings for the project*

Great! Now save your project wherever you prefer; I usually save it to my desktop. We can start exploring the Xcode functionalities!

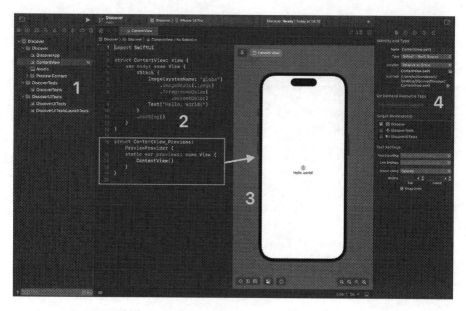

Figure 1-5. *Xcode – walk-through*

Xcode is composed of different tabs; each one has a different purpose:

1 – The left tab is showing all the files that your project contains. By default, there will be three main folders: One contains your app entry point named "*DiscoverApp*" like an index.html for the web developers. The *ContentView* comes by default; it is a starter template to present a user interface. Finally, there is an *Assets* folder that you can use to store your images and videos; this is useful since it will reduce the size of any assets that you upload. This folder will also contain your app logo.

The other two are for testing purposes. From there you can run tests to see if your code is robust or the user interface is responding accordingly. There is also a filter at the bottom to search through and a series of tabs at the top that will be useful when we are running the application.

2 – The second is where we are going to work! From there we can write code and see the content of our files. Also, in SwiftUI, every SwiftUI view comes with a struct called Preview (inside the green square). This is responsible to present you the screen on the right. If you delete this code, you won't be able to use the Canva feature.

3 – Canva has been introduced in 2019; it is an easy way to see the user interface that you are building live. From there, you can see how your app looks when you make changes in the code.

For example, try to add the keyword `.bold()` in the second panel right after the `Text("Hello, world!")`. Your text will turn to bold right away.

4 – The right tab is going to be your points of information for the file you are currently viewing. From there, you can rename it, change the programming language, and even edit some user interface elements, such as fonts and spacing between elements if you navigate to the last button at the top. Note that we won't be using this section much throughout the book.

Now, you can build your project. I invite you to click the build button, at the top left of Xcode as follows:

Figure 1-6. *Simulator running on Xcode*

Once you click it, a Simulator app will pop up and present you with a virtual iPhone running your application. You can also select other types of iPhones or iPads at the top panel so you can see how what you are building reacts to different screen sizes.

There are a lot of things to cover about Xcode. So far, what I highlighted are the main things to know and recognize, but we will discover more functionalities by coding. We will do just that in the next chapter and build our first application using Xcode and SwiftUI.

What Makes SwiftUI Different

SwiftUI has been introduced in 2019 by Apple at their WWDC; it is the declarative framework used by developers around the world to build applications for the Apple platforms. At the time of writing, we are at version 4.

SwiftUI makes you write better apps with less code as Apple states. Is it true? Prior to SwiftUI, we were using UIKit, an imperative framework introduced by Apple in 2014 to build user interfaces. It is still available, but it is slowly being replaced by Apple, since the company shifted the focus to SwiftUI.

To understand the evolution of these two frameworks, let's do a comparison by building two user interfaces composed of a list that displays elements from 1 to 10. For one of them, we will use UIKit, and the other will be built using SwiftUI. The user interface will look like this:

**List built with
SwiftUI & UIKit**

Figure 1-7. *A list displaying on an iPhone*

Observe the following code in UIKit:

```
import UIKit

class ViewController: UIViewController, UITableViewDelegate,
UITableViewDataSource {

    let tableView = UITableView()

    override func viewDidLoad() {
        super.viewDidLoad()
        view.addSubview(tableView)
        tableView.register(UITableViewCell.self,
        forCellReuseIdentifier: "Cell")
        tableView.dataSource = self
        tableView.delegate = self
    }

     override func viewDidLayoutSubviews() {
         super.viewDidLayoutSubviews()
         tableView.frame = view.bounds
    }
```

```swift
func tableView(_ tableView: UITableView,
numberOfRowsInSection section: Int) -> Int {
    return 10
}

func tableView(_ tableView: UITableView, cellForRowAt
indexPath: IndexPath) -> UITableViewCell {
    let cell = tableView.dequeueReusableCell(withIdentifier:
    "Cell", for: indexPath)
    cell.textLabel?.text = "\(indexPath.row)"
    return cell
}

}
```

As you can see, we import the framework UIKit at the top. We pass two delegates to our class: UITableViewDelegate and UITableViewDataSource. Then, we declare a UITableView to create the list that we manually added in the viewDidLoad method.

This method is being called when the view is being loaded, presented to the user. We also conform to this protocol with our two functions that return the numbers of rows and what they are composed of, here a cell with a text displaying the number of the current row.

Quite a bit of code to conform to the protocol and to present a basic user interface composed of ten rows.

Let's now code it using SwiftUI:

```swift
import SwiftUI

struct ContentView: View {
    var body: some View {
        List(0..<10) { index in
```

```
        Text("\(index)")
    }
  }
}
```

That's it! As you can see, with SwiftUI our list is way shorter. We import the framework at the top of the file. Then we directly declare a list in the *body* variable that contains 11 elements from zero to ten and its composition: a text displaying one to ten. It is literally two lines of code to create a *List*, much clearer and easier to read.

Now that we see that SwiftUI is much more efficient to build user interfaces, we are going to introduce a few bases. We will create a little application to introduce some APIs.

Coding with SwiftUI

To understand SwiftUI, the best thing to do is to build an application. So we are going to build a simple application that displays a few places on a map. Along with it, I will explain a few basics about SwiftUI.

Head to the Xcode project we created earlier called *Discover*. Run the application. You should have the following starter template:

Figure 1-8. *Xcode running with Simulator*

To recreate this screen, since it features Apple Maps, we need to import a framework called *MapKit* to access their APIs. So add the following line of code at the top of the file:

```
import MapKit
```

Then, right over the code *struct ContentView*, copy/paste the following code:

```
struct Place: Identifiable {
    var id = UUID()
    var title: String
    var coordinate: CLLocationCoordinate2D
    var architecte: String
}
```

We just implemented a model to create a few items from this model. Let me explain to you the code:

struct in Swift is used to store variables. Here we give the name of this struct: Place.

Identifiable is a protocol used to make this class identifiable. Since we are going to display the data in a *List*, we need to make each item identifiable.

Then, we give a few variables of type UUID to give a unique identifier, String for words, and CLLocationCoordinate2D to pass coordinates (latitude and longitude).

Great, we just created what is called a model, a modularization of our object (Place) with a few variables.

Now we can take care of our user interface.

Right under struct ContentView, add the following line of code:

```
@State private var region = MKCoordinateRegion(center: CLLocat
ionCoordinate2D(latitude: 41.9028, longitude: 12.4964), span:
MKCoordinateSpan(latitudeDelta: 0.1, longitudeDelta: 0.1))
```

What is the @State variable?

A property wrapper type that can read and write a value managed by SwiftUI.

—From the Apple documentation

This will allow us to manipulate data. Here we are passing coordinates that correspond to the coordinates of the city of Rome.

Then, we are declaring a constant, which contains an array of places. An array declared by [ ] is useful to present a series of data.

Copy/paste the following code right after the @State you declared earlier:

```
let annotations = [
        Place(title: "Fontana di Trevi", coordinate: CLLoc
        ationCoordinate2D(latitude: 41.900833, longitude:
        12.483056), architecte: "Nicola Salvi"),
        Place(title: "Pantheon", coordinate: CLLocationCoo
        rdinate2D(latitude: 41.8986, longitude: 12.4768),
        architecte: "Marcus Agrippa"),
        Place(title: "Villa Medici", coordinate: CLLocation
        Coordinate2D(latitude: 41.908, longitude: 12.483),
        architecte: "Bartolomeo Ammannati"),
        Place(title: "Colosseo",  coordinate: CLLocationCoor
        dinate2D(latitude: 41.890278, longitude: 12.492222),
        architecte: "Flavian Emperors")
    ]
```

Great, now we have all the necessary input to present locations on a *Map* and a few places to display.

Inside the body variable, replace the *VStack* with the following line of code:

```
Map(coordinateRegion: $region, annotationItems: annotations) {
            MapMarker(coordinate: $0.coordinate)
        }
```

This Map modifier will present a map in our application. We are passing a region parameter that we defined earlier with the coordinates of Rome, using the $ sign; it is the syntax to use with the *@State* variable. Also, we are adding annotations (the four places that we declared earlier).

To present these annotations, we are using *MapMarker* with the coordinates passed in our object.

If you correctly follow these short tutorials, you should have your Canva presenting a map with four annotations as follows:

Figure 1-9. *Our map application*

Summary

If you are new to Swift, this chapter has been useful to introduce you to Xcode, your tool to build applications for the Apple platform. Then, we saw the basics of Swift by creating a model and writing static data. Then, we used a map to display annotations, importing from the framework MapKit to access Apple's map APIs.

Now that we have a clearer idea of how to create a static model of data and present them, we can go ahead and talk about the backend. The next chapters will be focused on Firebase and how to download data from a backend, present them, modify them, and handle user input. Let's dive into the Firebase console.

Any source code or other supplementary material referenced by the author in this book is available to readers on the Github repository: https://github.com/Apress/Build-Mobile-Apps-with-SwiftUI-and-Firebase

CHAPTER 2

Introduction to Firebase

I am going to introduce you to the Firebase console and how to create a new project and connect an iOS application.

We will cover what is Firebase, why we are selecting this backend over others, and the advantages and disadvantages that come with it.

There is a walk-through to create your first Firebase project directly from the web browser. We are also going to connect our iOS application to talk to Firebase through its APIs.

By the end of this chapter, you will be able to create a new iOS app linked to the Firebase backend. For reference, please go to the Firebase documentation at the following link: `HTTPS://FIREBASE.GOOGLE.COM/DOCS/IOS/SETUP`.

What Is Firebase?

Firebase is what we call a backend as a service (BaaS), which means that rather than running your server to run your online applications, you pass through their services to read, write, update, and delete data, authenticate your users, and many more things!

Have a look at the following graphic that shows a native iOS application built with a custom backend running on the cloud:

© Sullivan De Carli 2023, corrected publication 2023
S. De Carli, *Build Mobile Apps with SwiftUI and Firebase*,
https://doi.org/10.1007/978-1-4842-9452-9_2

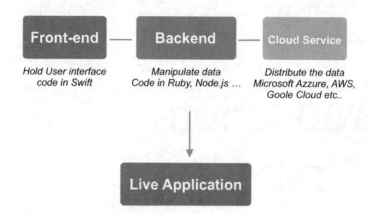

Figure 2-1. *An iOS app built with a backend host on a cloud service*

As you can see, the app will be communicating with a virtual machine usually coded in Ruby, Node.js, or PHP, itself hosted by a cloud service (which could also be physical, but it is rare nowadays) such as Amazon Web Services, Google Cloud Platform, Microsoft Azure, or whatever service. In complex applications with a large user base, it usually requires a frontend developer, in our case an iOS developer; a backend developer to develop the logic and the APIs; and finally a DevOps, responsible for bringing all of that to a cloud service and distributing it. A full-stack developer can also do it, but it is rare and requires a lot of experience.

Now, let's have a look at an iOS application built with Firebase:

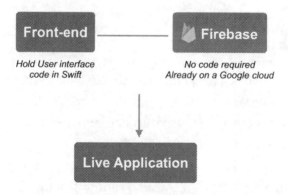

Figure 2-2. *An iOS app built with Firebase's backend*

As you see, the architecture is way easier. Our iOS is notifying and receiving data from Firebase using their APIs that come along with great documentation. There is no need to write code on the server side or host it to a third-party provider since it is already built on top of Google Cloud with no deployment needed by you! Additionally, you can still run backend code, thanks to the Firebase Cloud function, if you want to achieve more complex interactions later. In terms of a team, you need an iOS developer, and you're ready to publish an application on the App Store.

We have seen how much easier it is to use Firebase rather than running your backend code, but there is more: it comes with a series of out-of-the-box tools that help speed up your development.

For example, they have their APIs to authenticate a user with multiple third-party providers such as Apple, Facebook, Google, etc. They have Google Analytics preinstalled and ready to go.

Additionally, there are a series of extensions with third-party providers to sign up users to an email list, adding in-app purchase with RevenueCat with no code required.

You can discover them at this link:

HTTPS://FIREBASE.GOOGLE.COM/PRODUCTS/EXTENSIONS

Firebase comes with advantages and disadvantages. Here is the list: The pros:

- You are faster to ship your application. You don't need to write code on the backend unless you need to execute some more advanced functionalities.

- You have access to Google Cloud Platform with no operations needed on your side.

– You get out-of-the-box authenticate APIs with third parties. You don't need to use an API for Google sign-in and another one for Facebook sign-in, for example. You can pass directly through Firebase's APIs.

– You don't have to worry about scalability and managing servers.

The cons:

– The data don't belong to you to store them. The best thing to do is to run a snapshot of your data every day and store it in a secure place.

– You could be limited in some advanced applications where you need full control of the backend because the user interface is relying heavily on the backend.

Overall, Firebase is a great option if you want to release an application as fast as possible, the cheapest since you don't need to hire a backend developer. You can concentrate on what matters: building your product and monitoring the usage so you can implement features that your users want, which is also easier thanks to event follow-up and app analytics powered by Google Analytics that comes "for free."

That being said, let's discover Firebase, create our first project, and make our iOS app communicate with it.

Setting Up a Firebase Account and Project

To start on Firebase, you need to sign up for their services, which belong to Google, so you will need a Gmail account. If you don't already have one, sign up for a Gmail account first. Then go to the Firebase website (https://firebase.google.com), click "Get started," and you will be on your Firebase's console. You should see something like this:

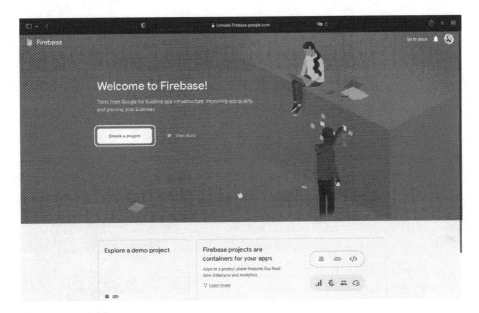

Figure 2-3. *Homepage of the Firebase console*

Click Create a project to create your first project on Firebase. I am going to guide you through every step, so you don't get lost on your way. It requires you to follow three straightforward steps.

Let's start with the first one:

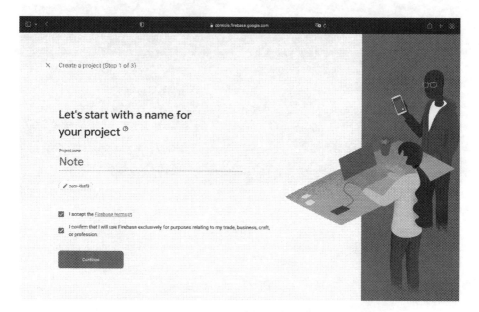

Figure 2-4. *Firebase new project, step 1 – project name*

For step 1, you just need to give it a name. I invite you to name it "Note" since it is the application we are going to build in the next chapter, but it doesn't matter.

The second step is to enable Google Analytics:

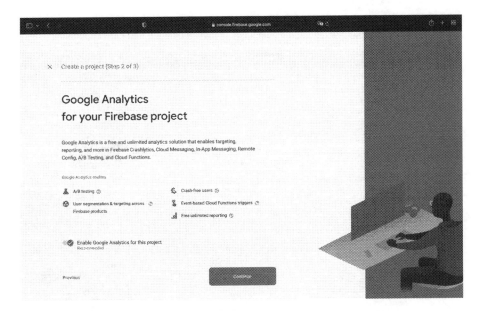

Figure 2-5. *Firebase new project, step 2 – Google Analytics*

This comes for free with Firebase, and it gives you access to basic data about how long your users are spending time on each screen, user usage over weeks, etc. You can even add events later to create funnels. For example, you will be able to find out how many users complete the signup process and then, for all those registered users, how many of them complete a purchase. For now, simply enable it and click Continue.

The third step looks like this screen:

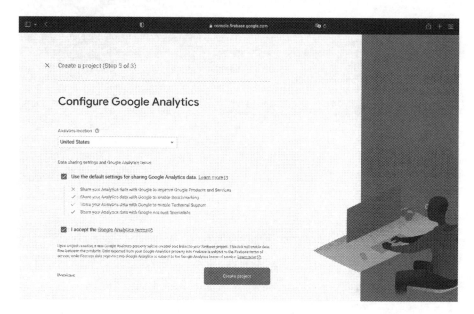

Figure 2-6. *Firebase new project, step 3 –Configure Google Analytics account*

For now, we can simply use the Firebase default account. If you have a website with Google Analytics tags to track usage and you want to build a related iOS application, you might want to select directly your Google Analytics account during this step. Click Create project, and you have created your first project on Firebase.

Firebase Walk-Through

You're now on the Firebase console. This is going to be the backbone of your application. Let me introduce it to you although we're going to dive in with our development in the next chapters.

Once the project is created, you will arrive at something like this:

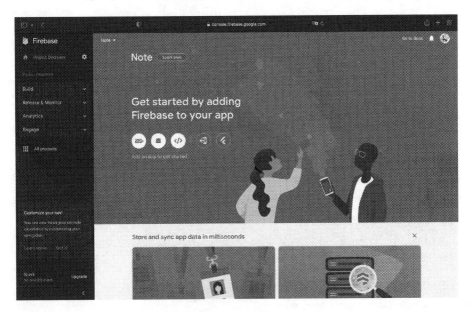

Figure 2-7. *The Firebase console*

This is a classic dashboard. In the left panel, you will get access to different menus categorized into four sections:

> Build – This is the place that we are going to explore the most. Here we will set up our authentication with third-party providers, create our database, and write our security rules and add extensions, a no-code solution.

> Release & Monitor – Once we have released our application on the App Store or even on TestFlight, you will be able to see reports if our users experienced crashes and even implement backend-powered distribution, which is not part of this book but good to have a look at because it is really powerful for iteration.

Analytics – From here you will have access to data usages of our app for free and implement some funnel from our code to monitor how a journey is being completed by our users.

Engage – This is especially powerful for stores and games. It offers features to send notifications with promotions, present advertisements with AdMob, and run A/B testing.

As you can imagine, there are a lot of features to cover with Firebase. For the scope of this book, you will be 90% of the time between Xcode and Firebase's Build section.

On the right, you have your Google account that you can switch as with every Google product and a "Go to docs" button. It is always good to refer to the documentation when you want to implement something or understand better how it works.

At the top, there is your project name. From there you can switch between projects.

The "Spark plan" label is your billing plan; this one is for free and comes with quite a lot of things. There is also the "pay as you go" connected to Google Cloud Platform. You will be billed based on your users' usages and the number of documents written and read.

For this book, the Spark plan will be enough although we might need to switch to pay as you go when we implement some extensions later because they run on Google Cloud Platform. It is going to be a few cents anyway since we are at a development stage.

It is now time to add our iOS application to talk to Firebase!

Connect Your iOS Application to Firebase

It's time to link our application to Firebase. To achieve this we will need to do some back-and-forth between Xcode and the Firebase console.

This walk-through is based on the Firebase documentation (`https://firebase.google.com/docs/ios/setup`). At the time of writing, the documentation doesn't include SwiftUI, so I recommend you follow it through.

First, we need to create a new Xcode project. Go ahead and click Create a new Xcode project:

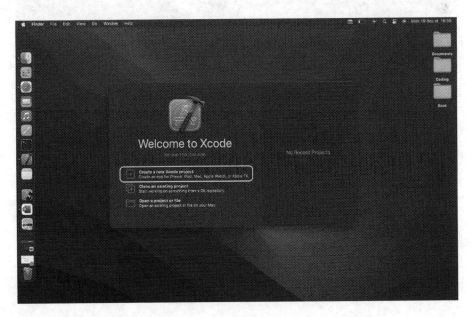

Figure 2-8. *Xcode – welcome screen*

Then, in terms of templates, it is going to be a classic application, so select the App template under the iOS platform:

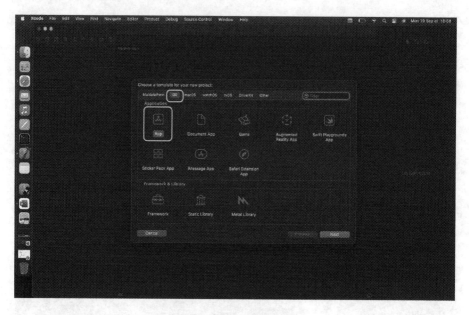

Figure 2-9. *Xcode – selecting an App template*

Finally, we need to give a name to our project. We will call it **Note** since this is the application we are building in the next chapter. Make sure to select SwiftUI for Interface. The use of Core Data is not required since we will have Firebase to store data:

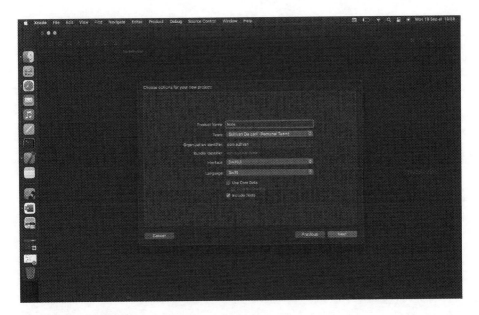

Figure 2-10. *Xcode – options for a new project*

You can save your project wherever you prefer. I saved it on my desktop. Now that our project is created, let's see how to connect it to Firebase. You can navigate back to the Firebase console. From the project overview, click iOS+ as follows:

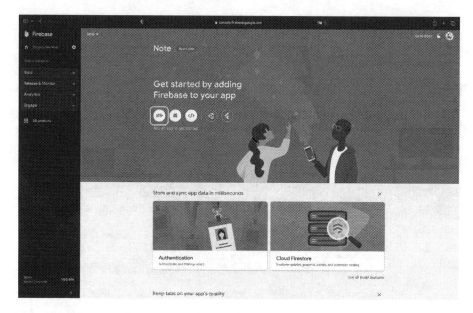

Figure 2-11. *Firebase console – adding an iOS app*

Firebase will present you a page inviting you to complete a five-step process, to connect your app to Firebase.

The first thing you need to do is to grab the Apple bundle ID. You will find it in Xcode on your main target. It is usually composed like the following:

com.[name of your team].[name of your project].

Please, check the following screenshot if you don't know where it is located:

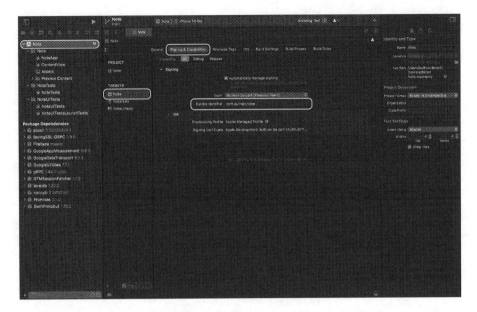

Figure 2-12. *Xcode – where to find the bundle identifier*

Once you have copied your identifier, you can copy/paste it. You also have the option to leave a nickname and the App Store ID, but these are optional:

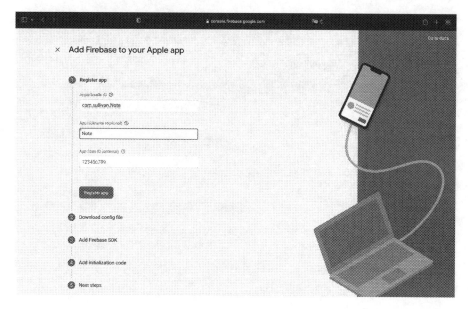

Figure 2-13. Add Firebase to your Apple app – step 1

Click Continue, and this will bring you to step 2, downloading the **GoogleService-Info.plist** file. Click the blue download button and save your file wherever you prefer. I saved it on my desktop:

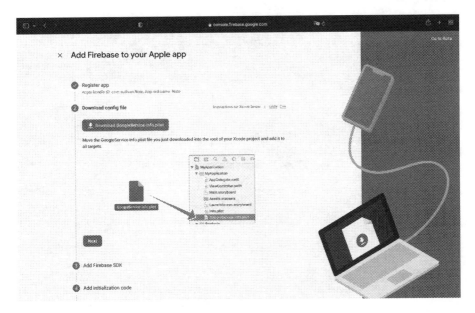

Figure 2-14. *Add Firebase to your Apple app – step 2*

Now that you have your file, you can drag and drop it to your Xcode folder from where you saved it. In my case, I dragged the file with my mouse directly to Xcode and then clicked the Finish button.

Make sure that Create folder references, Copy items if needed, and the target Note are selected

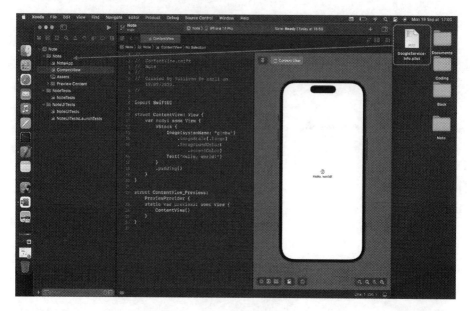

Figure 2-15. *Drag and drop the GoogleService-Info.plist file to Xcode*

Now that you have the file added to your project, Firebase will be able to recognize your app when you are making the APIs call it. You can now click Next.

You Might Be Wondering What This File Is For

The *GoogleService-Info.plist* is a file that contains all the information to communicate between your application and the Firebase backend; it contains the API key, the URL where your data will be collected, and a series of information to set up your project.

Make sure to add properly the file; otherwise, Firebase will not be able to find the essential information to connect to your iOS application and cause a crash when you call it.

In case you lose this file for some reason, you can always find it and download it from the Firebase console. Next to the project overview, there is a settings button. Click Project settings and then scroll down to SDK setup and configuration, and you will be able to download it again from there:

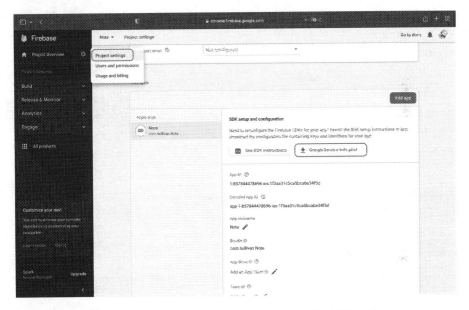

Figure 2-16. *Finding the GoogleService-Info.plist file in the console*

That being done, we can go to step 3 and install the *Firebase Software Development Kit (SDK)*. This can be achieved in multiple ways. The most popular are CocoaPods and Swift Package Manager. We will use the latter in our case.

You can copy the URL suggested by Firebase indicated in the following figure (`https://github.com/firebase/firebase-ios-sdk`):

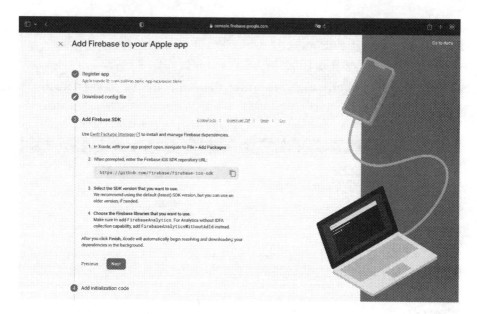

Figure 2-17. *Add Firebase to your apple app – step 3*

Once you have copied it, go back to Xcode and, at the top-left level, click File ➤ Add Packages…, and a pop-up screen will appear. Enter the URL you just copied into the search bar, and the *Firebase-ios-sdk* package should appear as in the following figure:

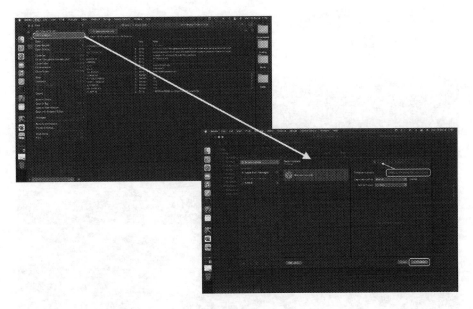

Figure 2-18. *Xcode – adding the package*

Note   Since I already added it to previous projects, it is already appearing under the section "Recently used."

Click the blue button at the bottom right called Add Package, and fetching will start and will propose you to add a product. For now, we will only use the three following packages:

- *FirebaseFirestore*

- *FirebaseFirestoreSwift*

- *FirebaseAuth*

Only these three modules will be necessary for our next chapters: replicating the Apple Notes app. However, for the following project, we will also be using Firebase Analytics, Firebase Storage, and more.

Once these three modules are selected, click Add Package again as in the following figure:

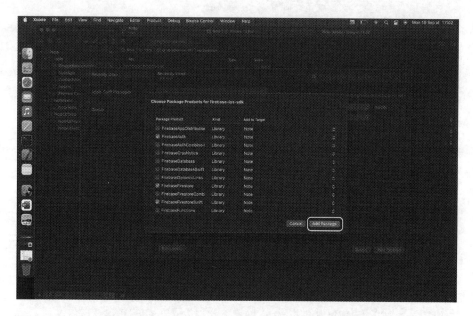

Figure 2-19. *Xcode ➤ Add Package – choosing products*

The installation will proceed for a few minutes depending on your Internet connection. Then you will see your project with the packages you installed, and you will be ready to use Firebase's APIs.

Let's move to step 4. In this step, we're going to initialize Firebase from our app main entry.

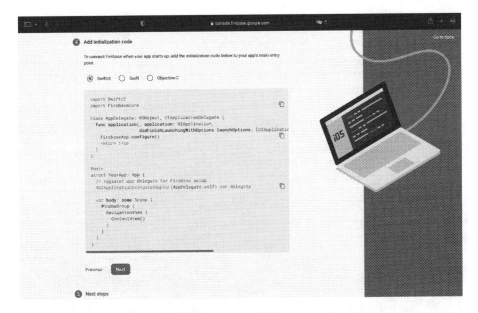

Figure 2-20. *Add Firebase to your Apple app – step 4*

Head to your file NoteApp.swift in Xcode and import Firebase at the top:

```
import FirebaseCore
```

Then, add the following code over the *@main* keyword:

```
class AppDelegate: NSObject, UIApplicationDelegate {
    func application(_ application: UIApplication,
    didFinishLaunchingWithOptions launchOptions:
    [UIApplication.LaunchOptionsKey : Any]? = nil) -> Bool {
        FirebaseApp.configure()
        return true
    }
}
```

Then add to following line of code inside the struct but over the body variable to register the App Delegate:

```
@UIApplicationDelegateAdaptor(AppDelegate.self) var delegate
```

Once you have implemented this code, your application will be able to communicate with Firebase. You can run your app (click the play button in the left tab), and you should have something like the following figure with the print in the console:

```
[boringssl] boringssl_metrics_log_metric_block_invoke(144)
Failed to log metrics
```

Figure 2-21. *Xcode running and communicating to Firebase*

Note   During the process, Xcode will be running quite a lot of modules from Firebase. If your MacBook is making a sound like an airplane at landing, it is normal; it is processing lots of files.

Congratulations! You have successfully set up Firebase to communicate with your app over an HTTP request, and you will now be able to use Firebase's APIs to use their amazing framework. You can now go ahead and click Continue to console:

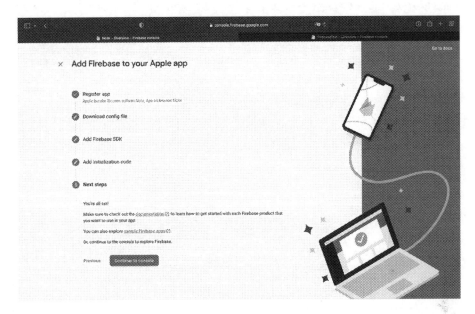

Figure 2-22.   *Add Firebase to your Apple app – step 5*

Summary

Over this chapter, we discovered what Firebase is and why we should consider it in our project development. We briefly explored the console and how to navigate the dashboard since we are going to dive in, in the next chapters.

Also, I walked you through how to create our first Firebase project and connect an iOS application using Swift Package Manager so you're ready to use their APIs.

Thanks to this setup, we are now ready to build our first working application and communicate data between Firebase and our application.

Any source code or other supplementary material referenced by the author in this book is available to readers on the Github repository: `https://github.com/Apress/Build-Mobile-Apps-with-SwiftUI-and-Firebase`

CHAPTER 3

Playing with Firestore

We are going to be focusing on Firebase Firestore over this chapter with a classic programming exercise: the Create-Read-Update-Delete (CRUD). Firestore is a NoSQL document-based database that will allow us to query, synchronize, and store data without managing infrastructure.

After introducing our app architecture and the MVVM design pattern, we will finally leave the "how it works" with the theory and the setup to the coding part by building an iOS application replicating the Apple Notes application that comes by default with Apple products. It is going to look like the following figure:

Figure 3-1. *Screenshots of the Note application we're going to build*

The app will feature a list of notes – we can delete a note directly from the main screen – a form to upload a new note, and a details screen to read it entirely, and we will have the ability to edit our notes.

By the end of this chapter, you will be able to properly structure your iOS project and make API calls to Firestore.

Introducing the MVVM Design Pattern

You might be wondering what is MVVM and what it stands for. MVVM is the short version for Model–View–View Model; it is an architecture widely used by the community of SwiftUI developers. Consider it as a *"how do I organize my code"* solution.

In Chapter 1, we played around with SwiftUI, and we kind of put all the pieces together without any structure. That's fine for an introduction. However, as our app becomes more complex, it can be unreadable and create conflicts in our code. That's where app architecture comes into place!

It will help us break down our code into multiples files. Each one has a specific purpose:

- The Model is responsible for structuring our data and holding the logic.

- The View Model will be responsible for managing the data, notified by the Model, and making the call to and from Firebase in our case.

- The View will present our user interface to our user: lists, buttons, text, images, and so on. It is going to be binding the data with our View Model.

You might be wondering why we need an architecture at all in our application. Well, it becomes important when you want to work on a project with more than one person and when the application becomes complex. It's preventing bugs in your code. Overall, it has these advantages:

- We will have a separation of concern. This way, each file has its own responsibility, and we avoid bugs and conflicts.

- It is easier to read and identify bugs. For example, if there is a UI problem, you must look in your View; if there is an HTTP request problem, the View Model is the file to look for. Missing a data? You might have to add it inside the Model.

Now, take a moment to see the following graphic showing the design pattern:

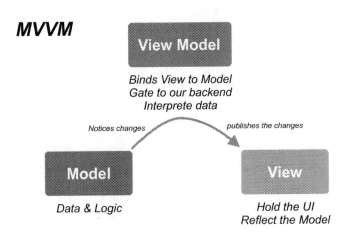

Figure 3-2. MVVM architecture in graphic

As you can see, the Model is communicating with the View Model, responsible to interpret the data and pass them to the View, which is solely responsible for presenting the user interface and notifying also the View Model about users' intent.

For example, in our application that we are going to build, the Model will be composed of an identifier and a title. This structure will be notifying the View Model responsible for making the read call to Firebase and then presenting the data inside our View in a list.

What happens when the data flows the other way?

If it is from the View to the Model through the View Model, the View will notify the View Model, which will interpret this action and then modify the Model. For example, when a user deletes a note, the View will notify the View Model, which will inform Firebase to delete that document based on the information structured in our Model.

Now, if this still sounds abstract to you, do not worry. By practicing it in our application during this chapter, it will be clearer to you.

Create Data to Firestore

Before we start coding, Firebase still needs a bit of setup to work with the Firestore database. Go to your Firebase console and head to the Firestore Database section in the left panel and click the Create database button as in the following figure:

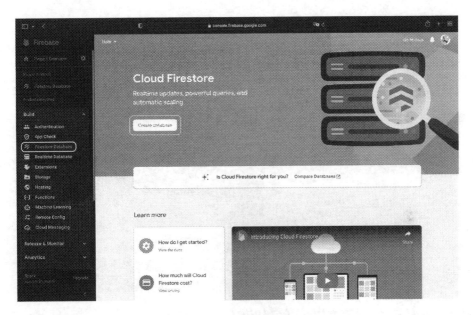

Figure 3-3. *Firebase console – Firestore section*

A pop-up will appear inviting you to complete a two-step process. The first one is to choose how to start your database. We will go ahead with test mode, since we are only discovering Firebase in this chapter. We don't need to set up rules to restrict our Firebase usage to authenticated users, for example. Additionally, we are on the Spark plan, and we didn't enter a credit card yet, so we are good to go regarding billing.

The second step is to select a location. Simply choose the one closer to you. I picked up US-Central, but if you're going to distribute the app for the European market, it is better to select Central Europe as the database since it is going to be closer and slightly more efficient. Follow the two steps as described in the following:

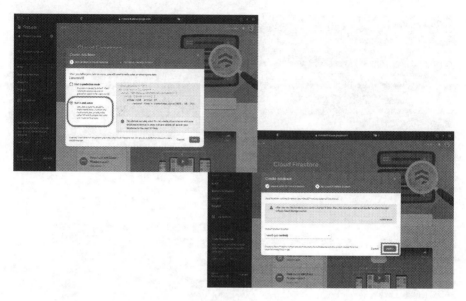

Figure 3-4. *Firestore two-step setup*

Now that our database is activated, it's time to get back to Xcode. Open the project Note that we created and connected to Firebase earlier.

According to the MVVM architecture we spoke about earlier, we are going to create the Model.

Click Create a new file ➤ Swift File and call it *Note*. Then paste the following code:

```swift
import Foundation
import FirebaseFirestoreSwift

struct Note: Codable {
    @DocumentID var id: String?
    var title: String?
}
```

That's all we need for our Model, an identifier and a title that will hold the text we will enter later in our form.

Note here that we have imported *FirebaseFirestoreSwift* to access the @*DocumentID* keyword; this comes from Firebase to help us map the document correctly with the identifier from Firebase.

The next step is to create our View Model. This file will be responsible for passing data to our View conforming to the Model we just created. It's also going to talk to Firebase using their APIs, so we need to import the Firestore framework at the top.

Click Create a new file ➤ Swift File and name it *NoteViewModel* and import the framework at the top:

```
import FirebaseFirestore
```

You can then copy/paste the following code into your file:

```
class NoteViewModel: ObservableObject {

    @Published var notes = [Note]()
    private var databaseReference = Firestore.firestore().
    collection("Notes")

    // function to post data

    // function to read data

    // function to update data

    // function to delete data

}
```

Great, we just created a class conforming to the *ObservableObject*; it allows instances of this class to be used inside views later, so when changes happen, the View will reload with the updated changes.

Then, we have created a reference to our Model with the *Published* to tell our program to reload when changes happen with our Model.

Also, we added a variable so we can refer to the Firestore collection that we just named Notes. It is useful to add this reference, so we don't need to write it multiple times when we are writing a function to fetch, read, delete, or update data.

It is now time to add the function to post data to Firestore right under a comment I left:

```
// function to post data
    func addData(title: String) {
        do {
            _ = try databaseReference.addDocument
            (data: ["title": title])
        }
        catch {
            print(error.localizedDescription)
        }
    }
```

There is not much to comment on here. We are using the *addDocument* APIs from Firebase passing our data: the title as a string. It's also catching errors in case there are some; it is going to be printed in our console with the catch.

That's enough for our Model–View Model to post data to Firestore. It's now time to build our user interface. We are going to create the UI for our form and handle the logic to present it from our ContentView.swift file.

Go ahead and click Create a new file ➤ SwiftUI View and call it *FormView*:

```
import SwiftUI

struct FormView: View {

    @Environment(\.dismiss) var dismiss
    @State var titleText = ""
```

```
var body: some View {
    // ...
}
```

These lines of code will be helpful to handle the presentation and handle the text entry of our user with a title.

Now let's build a form. Add the following code inside the body variable:

```
NavigationStack {
        Form {
            Section {
                TextEditor(text: $titleText)
                    .frame(minHeight: 200)
            }
            Section {
                Button(action: {
                    //TODO: upload data
                }) {
                    Text("Save now")
                }.disabled(self.titleText.isEmpty)
                    .foregroundColor(.yellow)
            }
        }.navigationTitle("Publish")
            .toolbar {
                ToolbarItemGroup(placement:
                .destructiveAction) {
                    Button("Cancel") {
                        dismiss()
                    }
                }
            }
    }
```

Great! We just added a *NavigationStack* with a form composed of a TextEditor (better than *TextField* for long entries). Also, we added a button to publish, which is disabled if there is no text entry, and another button as part of the navigation at the top to dismiss it.

We can now call this screen from the *ContentView.swift* file! Add the followings *@State* to observe the presentation:

```swift
import SwiftUI

struct ContentView: View {

    @State private var showingSheet = false @State private var
    postDetent = PresentationDetent.medium

    var body: some View {
        // ...
    }
}

struct ContentView_Previews: PreviewProvider {
  // ...
}
```

It's now time to create our bottom bar with the button to present our form modally.

Add the following code inside the body variable:

```swift
NavigationStack {
        List {
        // TODO: present our notes
            }
        .toolbar {
            ToolbarItemGroup(placement: .bottomBar) {
                Text(" X notes") // TODO
                Spacer()
```

```
Button {
    // Write a new note
    showingSheet.toggle()
} label: {
    Image(systemName: "square.and.pencil")
}
  .imageScale(.large)
  .sheet(isPresented: $showingSheet) {
    FormView().presentationDetents
    ([.large, .medium])
}
    }
} }.navigationTitle("Notes")
```

We just added another *NavigationStack* with a list that we are going to fill out with data in the next section and a button at the bottom replicating the one from the Apple Notes app, thanks to SF Symbols.

> *SF Symbols is a library of icons built by Apple. As of now, it provides over 4, 400 symbols. This way, you don't need designer skills to integrate nice-looking icons into your application. If you want to check out what icons you can pick up, you can download Apple's application at the following page:*
>
> `https://developer.apple.com/sf-symbols/.`

This sheet will be presented upon button tap and can be dismissed from the form.

You can run your application and check the interaction; you should be able to access the form and close it multiple times.

Now that we are good to go with our user interface, it's time to post data to Firestore and head to *FormView* again.

And add the following observer just over the body variable:

```
@ObservedObject private var viewModel = NoteViewModel()
```

This will make the data binding between our View and our View
Model. Now we only need to call the function we created earlier inside our
button action, where we left the *TODO: upload data* comment, as follows:

```
var body: some View {

  NavigationStack {
          Form {
              Section {
                  // ..
              }
              Section {
                  Button(action: {
                          self.viewModel.addData(title:
                          titleText)
                  titleText = ""
                  dismiss()
                      }) {
                          // ..
                      }
                      // ...
              }
          }.navigationTitle("Publish")
              // ...
      }
}
```

Et voilà! We simply recall our function from the View Model to publish
data to Firebase, passing the content of the title text. Then we dismiss the
View with *dismiss()*.

Run your application, write some texts, and click "Save now."

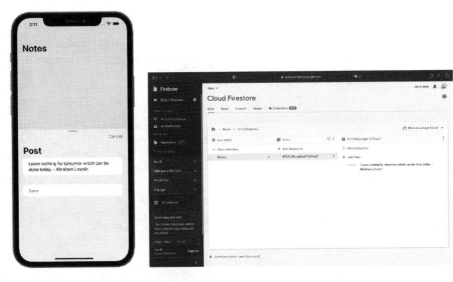

Figure 3-5. *Uploading data to Firestore*

Let's see what's happens on your Firebase Firestore console:

Congratulations! We just did our first call with Firebase's APIs, adding a document under the Notes collection. You can even go ahead and add as many as you want!

It's now time to read these notes and display them inside our list!

Read Data from Firestore

It is now time to read our notes since we have posted a few on Firestore. Inside our *ContentView.swift* file, we added a *NavigationView*, composed of a *List*. We will display the data in this list, but we haven't added the function to fetch these data. It's time to head to the *NoteViewModel.swift* file and add the following function under the comment that we left:

```
// function to read data
  func fetchData() {
```

```
databaseReference.addSnapshotListener { (querySnapshot,
error) in
    guard let documents = querySnapshot?.
    documents else {
        print("No documents")
        return
    }

    self.notes = documents.compactMap {
    queryDocumentSnapshot -> Note? in
        return try? queryDocumentSnapshot.data
        (as: Note.self)
    }
  }
}
```

This function to read data from Firestore was missing. It is adding a listener so our frontend can receive updates from our backend in real time based on the Model *Note* we have created.

Let's use it in our *ContentView* now to fetch the data and display them in a list. As we did in the *FormView*, we need to also observe our *View Model*. Please add the following line of code, over the body variable inside our *ContentView.swift* file:

```
@ObservedObject private var viewModel = NoteViewModel()
```

Now that we are ready to listen to the updates from our View Model, let's implement the UI now (still in the *ContentView.swift* file):

```
import SwiftUI

struct ContentView: View {

    // ...
```

```swift
var body: some View {

NavigationStack {
        List {
        ForEach(viewModel.notes, id:\.id) { Note in
            VStack(alignment: .leading) {
                Text(Note.title ?? "").font(.
                system(size: 22, weight: .regular))
            }.frame(maxHeight: 200)

        }
        }.onAppear(perform: self.viewModel.fetchData)
    .toolbar {
        ToolbarItemGroup(placement: .bottomBar) {
            Text("\(viewModel.notes.count) notes")
            Spacer()
            Button {
                // ...
            } label: {
                Image(systemName: "square.and.pencil")
            }
             // ...
        }
    }
    }
}.navigationTitle("Notes")

// ..
```

We just implemented a list based on our Model, attributing to each one an identifier; otherwise, when we add or delete notes, SwiftUI wouldn't be able to know what to refer to. That's what this id:\.id is for.

Also, we are fetching the data with the .OnAppear modifier, so the function is called anytime the View appears.

We also added the code `viewModel.notes.count` to let the user know how many notes there are registered on our application, similar to Apple's Notes application.

Run the app, and all the data you added will be there. I added a few quotes from the US presidents. My list looks like this:

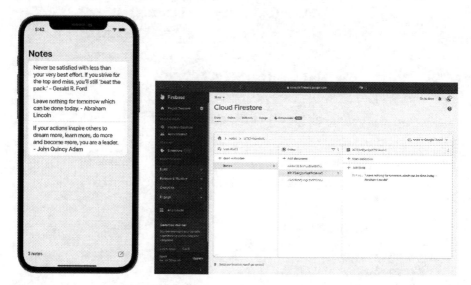

Figure 3-6. *Reading data from Firestore*

Pass Data from Views

Now, what if we want to read the entire quote? Not easy from the list. It might be cool to present another screen with more details. That's what we are going to implement. The challenge here is to pass the data between views with the correct identifier. Let's do that.

We are going to create a *DetailsView* to present our text in a *ScrollView* so we can read the whole text.

Create a new SwiftUI View file and call it "*DetailsView*" and add the following code to it:

```
import SwiftUI

struct DetailsView: View {

    var note: Note

    var body: some View {
        Text("\(note.title ?? "")")
    }
}

struct DetailsView_Previews: PreviewProvider {
    static var previews: some View {
 DetailsView(note: Note(id: "bKrivNkYirmMvHyAUBWv", title:
 "Issues are never simple. One thing I'm proud of is that very
 rarely will you hear me simplify the issues.Barack Obama"))
    }
}
```

This way, we have a reference to pass the data from the ContentView to our DetailsView. Also, we need to init inside our preview with some default data; otherwise, Xcode won't let us run our application.

We also replace the Text "Hello, world" with our note's title, passing a default empty string in case there is no data with ?? "".

It's now time to make the row clickable and pass the data. Let's head back to the *ContentView* file and embed the *VStack* with your text in a *NavigationLink* modifier as follows:

```
struct ContentView: View {

    // ...

    var body: some View {
        NavigationStack {
```

```
            List(viewModel.notes, id: \.id) { Note in
                NavigationLink(destination: DetailsView(note:
                Note)) {
                    VStack(alignment: .leading) {
                        Text(Note.title ?? "").font(.
                        system(size: 22, weight: .regular))
                    }.frame(maxHeight: 200)
                } }
            }.onAppear(perform: self.viewModel.fetchData)
        }
.toolbar {
        // ...
        }
    }.navigationTitle("Notes")
} }
```

And this is all that we need. With SwiftUI's NavigationLink, we just need to pass which views we want to present and the data they need to contain. Here we refer to the Note Model that we have also called inside the *DetailsView* to make it work.

Note that the `NavigationLink` only works inside a `NavigationView` as it is part of the protocol.

You can now run your app and click a row; it will open the `DetailsView` and present you the details based on the row you clicked.

But let's improve a bit our user interface for our *DetailsView*. We will give a title to the navigation bar, and we will place our text inside a *ScrollView* so we can read it entirely when the text is long. Implement the following code inside the body variable:

```
NavigationStack {
        ScrollView {
            VStack {
```

```
        Text(note.title ?? "")
            .font(.system(size: 22, weight:
            .regular))
            .padding()

        Spacer()
    }
}

}.navigationTitle("Details")
```

That is nicer! We are now conforming to our initial user interface:

Figure 3-7. *Navigating from a list to another view*

Thanks to the NavigationLink, a > symbol appears automatically in our row, indicating to our user that it is clickable. Now, what if we miswrite a note? Let's implement an editor for that!

Update Data from Firestore

In this section, we will implement a new screen to edit a note and save that text entry to Firestore. But first, let's head to our View Model and add the necessary functionality to update it to Firestore.

Paste the following code in NoteViewModel.swift:

```
// function to update data
    func updateData(title: String, id: String) {
        databaseReference.document(id).updateData(["title" :
        title]) { error in
            if let error = error {
                print(error.localizedDescription)
            } else {
                print("Note updated successfully")
            }
        }
    }
```

As you can see, we are passing an identifier inside our document to let Firestore know which document needs to be updated. Then, we pass the title to be modified inside the updateData function. As usual, we print the errors if there are any.

Time for the user interface. We will use an alert presentation with a TextField to let the user update the text. Add the following code at the top of DetailsView:

```
@State private var presentAlert = false
@State private var titleText: String = ""
@ObservedObject private var viewModel =   NoteViewModel()
```

We will need these parameters for our interaction:

- @State as a Boolean to handle the presentation of our alert

- @State to follow the entry of our TextField

And, of course, our View Model informs it from our View to be updated.

We are good to go to present our Alert from our DetailsView. First, we need to add a button "Edit" to this screen; we will do this with a toolbar. You can add it right under the navigationTitle:

```
.toolbar {
            ToolbarItemGroup(placement:
            .confirmationAction) {
                Button {
                    presentAlert = true
                } label: {
                    Text("Edit").bold()
                }.alert("Note", isPresented: $presentAlert,
                actions: {
                    TextField("\(note.title ?? "")", text:
                    $titleText)
                    Button("Update", action: {
                    //TODO: Update data and erase the text
                    })
                    Button("Cancel", role: .cancel,
                    action: {
```

```
                        presentAlert = false
                        titleText = ""
                    })
                }, message: {
                    Text("Write your new note")
                })
            }
        }
```

Great! Now we can present our Alert, passing data along the way. We can now add our function to update our notes. Add the following code where we left the // TODO: comment, in the DetailsView:

```
self.viewModel.updateData(title: titleText, id: note.id ?? "")
titleText = ""
```

Et voilà! We are now ready to run our app and edit our notes. The field that we enter will now populate the note selected with the appropriate identifier.

Let's say you want to change the citation from Abraham Lincoln

"Leave nothing for tomorrow which can be done today. - Abraham Lincoln"

to another quote from Barack Obama:

"Change will not come if we wait for some other person, or if we wait for some other time. - Barack Obama"

Go ahead to your list, navigate to details, and click the Edit button. Then enter the preceding text. You will see that the text is going to be updated in the DetailsView and then inside our List:

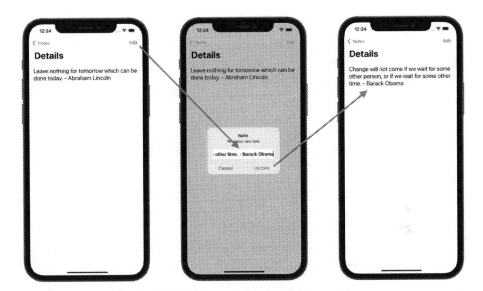

Figure 3-8. *Editing a note from our Simulator*

We are now editing a note, and it's edited in real time on our backend and in our user interface.

Now, what if you want to delete a note? Let's implement our last feature.

Delete Data from Firestore

Let's implement our last step: deleting the data from Firestore. We left a mark in our NoteViewModel just for that. Head to this file and add the following code:

```
// function to delete data
    func deleteData(at indexSet: IndexSet) {
        indexSet.forEach { index in
            let note = notes[index]
            databaseReference.document(note.id ?? "").delete {
            error in
```

```
            if let error = error {
                print("\(error.localizedDescription)")
            } else {
                print("Note with ID \(note.id ?? "")
                deleted")
            }
        }
    }
}
```

In the delete function, we are giving an `indexSet`, useful to have a reference to our list, and then passing the identifier that we created in our Model so we are passing the correct ID information to Firestore to delete the right document (the one selected in the row). As always, we are printing the error if there is any, and we are printing the document identifier if it's successful.

Now let's make it happen on screen! Head to the `ContentView.swift` file:

```
struct ContentView: View {

    // ...

var body: some View {
        NavigationStack {
            List {
                ForEach(viewModel.notes, id:\.id) { Note in
                    NavigationLink(destination:
                    DetailsView(note: Note)) {
                      // ...
                    }
                }.onDelete(perform: self.viewModel.
                deleteData(at:))
```

```
        }.onAppear(perform: self.viewModel.fetchData)
            .navigationTitle("Notes")
    }
        .toolbar {
            // ...
    }
    }.navigationTitle("Notes")
} }
```

That's it! It is super easy to delete an item from a list using SwiftUI. The onDelete modifier handles the swipe left with a Delete title and a red background. Our function will do the rest to delete the document on Firestore.

Now I invite you to run your application on the Simulator. Swipe left on a row you wish to delete, and check out what's happening on your Firestore console:

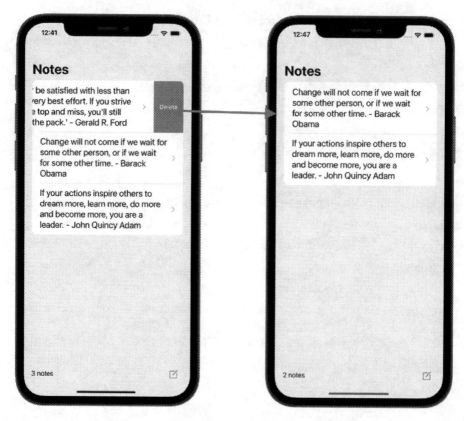

Figure 3-9. *Deleting a note from the list and Firestore database*

By doing this, you will see a deletion occurring on the backend in real time. Then your note will disappear from the list, and our number of notes will be updated inside the toolBar.

Summary

We have completed our first Note app with feature functions present in most applications: the ability to post, read, update, and delete content to and from a backend. This was a nice CRUD exercise and a great way to get you started with SwiftUI and Firebase.

In this chapter, we covered how to structure our app using the MVVM design pattern and the first use of Firebase's APIs and set up a cloud Firestore database and make things work between our user interface and our backend or, better, between our View Model and our backend.

In the following, you will find the link to the repository of this first application. In case you missed something on the way, check out the repository:

How to use this repository? If you clone this repository and run your application, it will crash. Why? Because there is no *GoogleService-Info.plist* file in this project. Firebase will look for it and not find the necessary API key and so not be able to initiate and cause the crash.

To make it work, you will need to go to your Firebase console, add a new iOS project as we did in Chapter 2, pass the correct bundle identifier, and add the *GoogleService-Info.plist* to this project. These two steps are crucial for making the app run properly. Normally, the packages should fetch themselves with SPM, so you can skip this step.

It's now time to head to the next chapter: we will discover Firebase Auth and authenticate our first user!

Any source code or other supplementary material referenced by the author in this book is available to readers on the Github repository: `https://github.com/Apress/Build-Mobile-Apps-with-SwiftUI-and-Firebase`

CHAPTER 4

Authenticate Users with Firebase Auth

We are going to be focusing on Firebase Auth SDK over this chapter. We are going to create an authentication flow that grants us access to our Create-Read-Update-Delete (CRUD) functionalities that we implemented earlier. We will perform this thanks to the Firebase authenticate API to validate credentials against their response from the server. We will also use Firestore to store user information in a collection (similar to tables in the SQL kind of databases).

Then we will restrict the access to users with an account only like onboarding in applications like Twitter, Instagram, etc. For this, we will need to listen to the status of the user that Firebase provides us.

Firebase Auth SDK allows us to know when a user is logged in or logged out, thanks to their listener APIs. These are the screens we are going to build:

© Sullivan De Carli 2023, corrected publication 2023
S. De Carli, *Build Mobile Apps with SwiftUI and Firebase*,
https://doi.org/10.1007/978-1-4842-9452-9_4

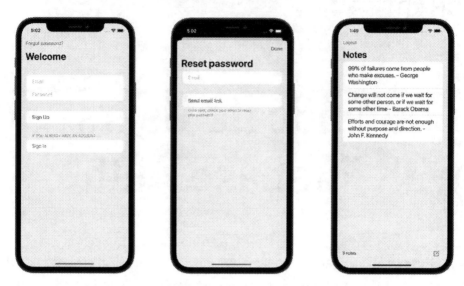

Figure 4-1. *Screenshots of the screens we are going to create*

At the end, we will also edit the security rules to allow only authenticated users to have access to our application.

Setting Up Firebase Authenticate

The first thing to do is to set up Firebase in our dashboard. We will head to the console to enable authentication. It will take us only a few steps. For this, select the Authentication section and click "Get started":

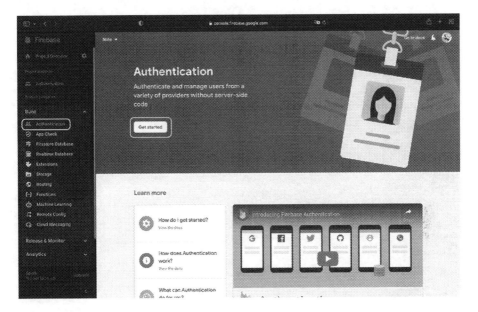

Figure 4-2. *Firebase console Authentication section*

As you can see, Firebase offers many options to authenticate users. It natively supports email with password, phone authentication, and anonymous, which allows you to generate a unique identifier for your users without requiring them to enter any information.

Regarding the third parties, there are plenty of options between the bigger tech providers: Facebook, Google, Apple, Microsoft, Twitter, GitHub, Yahoo, and more. We will implement one of these in one of the next chapters.

For this application, we will only use email and password to get started. Select Email/Password under Native providers:

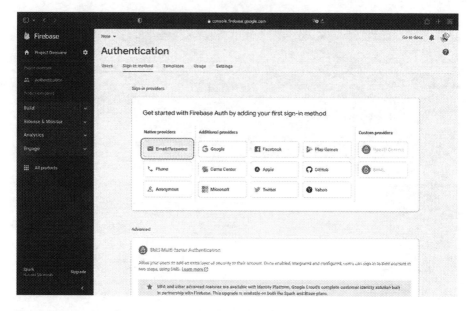

Figure 4-3. *Authentication – selection of Email/Password*

Then, simply enable it and save the changes:

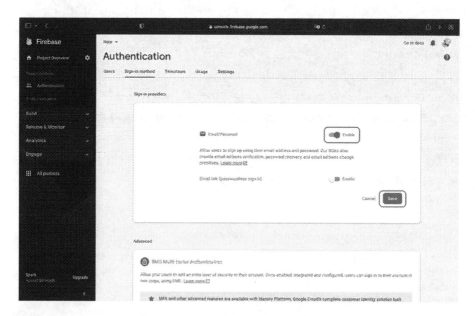

Figure 4-4. *Authentication – enabling the provider and saving*

Now, you can send users' information to register our users and receive back responses from their servers. It's now time to structure our code and implement the Firebase APIs. Let's code!

Manage User Sessions

Let's build our call to Firebase to listen to changes in users' sessions. Let's go ahead and create a new file. Let's call it *AuthViewModel*; it is going to be our View Model to communicate with Firebase Authenticate.

Copy/paste the code as follows:

```
import SwiftUI
import FirebaseAuth

final class AuthViewModel: ObservableObject {
  @Published var user: User?

func listenToAuthState() {
    Auth.auth().addStateDidChangeListener { [weak self]
    _, user in
      guard let self = self else {
        return
      }
      self.user = user
    }
  }
// function to sign-in

// function to create an account

// function to logout

// function to reset password

}
```

Please, note that we won't be using a model this time.

We will directly pass through the User object that Firebase Auth SDK provided us called FIRUser. It provides a series of information: a displayName, a picture URL, an email, a phone number, and a provider identifier.

Since we are using email/password, we will only need the email and an identifier. It allows us to not write the Model ourselves. We only made a reference with this line of code:

```
@Published var user: User?
```

For now, we added a reference to our user model and a function to take information from Firebase *listenToAuthState()*. This will be useful to determine if we need to present the list of notes or the signup view from the response we obtain from Firebase.

The first thing to do is to create two SwiftUI views to handle both cases. Go ahead and create two files. Call these screens with the following names:

- *SignUpView* (where we enter the credentials)

- *HolderView* (where we will implement the logic)

This is the representation of the logic we are going to implement:

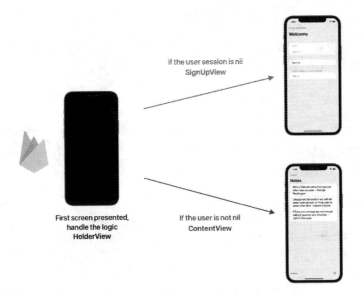

Figure 4-5. *Logic implemented with the Firebase Auth listener*

To perform this logic, we need to add this View Model as an environment object at the start-up of our app, the `NoteApp.swift` file (the starting point of our application), inside the body variable.

The @environmentObject property from SwiftUI allows us to share data between views and ensure that our views get automatically updated based on what they receive.

Here, we need to inform our app entry the state of the user session, so we can present the right screen at the right moment.

Head to the *NoteApp* file, and instead of ContentView(), we will add the following line of code:

```
HolderView().environmentObject(AuthViewModel())
```

What is this for? It will allow us to notify our application upon start-up (when a user opens for the first time, after killing the app or whatever) that we are binding this to the View Model, so we are able to use the snapshot listener implemented here and present the correct screen based on the user's session.

Now, we will head to the HolderView to incorporate the logic.

First, let's observe our View Model in the HolderView. Copy/paste the following *@EnvironmentObject* variable:

```
@EnvironmentObject private var authModel: AuthViewModel
```

And now, let's implement the conditional statement to present the appropriate view based on the Firebase response. Inside the *body* variable, instead of the current

```
Text("Hello, World!")
```

paste the following code:

```
Group {
        if authModel.user == nil {
            SignUpView()
        } else {
            ContentView()
        }
    }
    .onAppear {
        authModel.listenToAuthState()
    }
```

Now, run the application, and you should have the following:

Figure 4-6. *Xcode – app running with the Auth listener*

Great! As you can see, we have the *SignUpView* presented at start-up. It makes sense because Firebase is returning nil when we ask for a user because we didn't sign up any yet.

Now that we have implemented the logic, we can go ahead and sign up our user. Let's create the user interface to sign up and implement the function.

Sign Up with Email and Password

First things first, let's build the user interface. We are going to add two fields – one for the email and one for the password – and two buttons: one for signing up and one for signing in.

To achieve this, we are going to use a form since it comes with a scrolling feature for free and it is faster to implement.

Head to our *AuthViewModel,* and implement the API calls to sign in, sign up and sign out:

```
// function to sign-in
func signIn(
        emailAddress: String,
        password: String
    ) {
        Auth.auth().signIn(emailAddress: emailAddress,
        password: password) { result, error in
            if let error = error {
                print("an error occurred: \(error.
                localizedDescription)")
                return
            }
        }
    }

// function to create an account
func signUp(
        emailAddress: String,
        password: String
    ) {
        Auth.auth().createUser(withEmail: emailAddress,
        password: password) { result, error in
            if let error = error {
                print("an error occurred: \(error.
                localizedDescription)")
                return
            }
        }
    }
```

```
// function to logout
    func signOut() {
        do {
            try Auth.auth().signOut()
        } catch let signOutError as NSError {
            print("Error signing out: %@", signOutError)
        }
    }
```

Great, we just implemented the necessary functions; the syntax of the APIs is quite clear here. We are using sign-in and creating a user and passing an email and password object as part of the parameter.

To log out, we are using a do, try catch to catch any errors in case there is a bad Internet connection, for example.

Head to the *SignUpView*, and implement the following code:

```
@State private var emailAddress: String = ""
@State private var password: String = ""
```

These two variables will allow us to observe the user's input and pass it to the Firebase backend. Now, let's implement the user interface and replace the current:

```
NavigationStack {
        Form {
            Section {
                TextField("Email", text: $emailAddress)
                    .textContentType(.emailAddress)
                    .keyboardType(.emailAddress)
                SecureField("Password", text: $password)
            }

            Section {
                Button(action: {
```

```
                      // Sign Up to Firebase
              }) {
                  Text("Sign Up").bold()
              }
          }
          Section(header: Text("If you already have an
account:")) {

              Button(action: {
                  // Sign In to Firebase
              }) {
                  Text("Sign In")
              }
          }
      }.navigationTitle("Welcome")
          .toolbar {
              ToolbarItemGroup(placement:
              .cancellationAction) {
                  Button {
                      showingSheet.toggle()
                  } label: {
                      Text("Forgot password?")
                  }
                  .sheet(isPresented: $showingSheet) {
                      ForgotPasswordView()
                  }
              }
          }
      }
  }
```

Great, now we have our user interface. It's time to pass the email and password to Firebase. Let's observe the View Model we created earlier:

```
@EnvironmentObject private var authModel: AuthViewModel
```

And let's implement the signup function inside the button action that belongs to the signup button:

```
authModel.signUp(emailAddress: emailAddress,
                             password: password)
```

And let's do the same thing for the sign-in process – add the function inside the button action:

```
authModel.signIn(emailAddress: emailAddress,
                 password: password)
```

It is now time to sign up our first user. Go ahead, run your application, enter an email and a password, and check out the Firebase console!

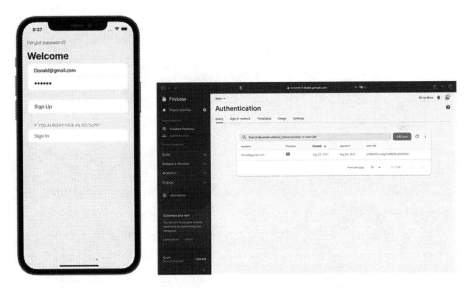

Figure 4-7. *App running and posting user data to Firebase Authenticate*

Great! By entering an email and a password, our app is notified in real time that the user has an active session. Then, it automatically brings us to the main screen, the ContentView.

But what about signing out the user? This time, we also need to update our user interface and bring back our user to the signup screen. Also, giving the ability to log out will grant us the ability to log in again on the same device and check if our sign-in function is working properly.

Let's add this logout button and execute the sign-out function.

Observe the *AuthViewModel* at the top of the ContentView.swift file:

```
@ObservedObject private var authModel = AuthViewModel()
```

Then, right below the first ToolbarItemGroup and inside the graph of the .toolbar modifier, add the following:

```
ToolbarItemGroup(placement: .cancellationAction) {
            Button {
                authModel.signOut()
            } label: {
                Text("Logout")
            }
        }
```

Really simple. Since we added all the functions in the View Model, we only need to call them in the user interface.

Go ahead and click the logout button. You will be brought back to the signup screen. It's now time to try the sign-in function. Enter the email and password you used earlier.

You can perform the action many times and create as many accounts as you want to see the robustness of the code. That's it. We have a fully functioning login flow!

What If You Forget Your Password?

That can happen often, especially nowadays, where we have so many accounts to manage. Thankfully, Firebase provides us with an API to reset the password and even send an email on our behalf! Great, isn't it?

We just need to pass an email address from the frontend.

To achieve this, we will create a new screen to reset the password.

So go ahead and create a new SwiftUI View and call it ResetPasswordView; we will call this *view* from our SignUpView as a pop-up.

Before implementing the user interface, we will implement the function to reset our password, so head to *AuthViewModel* and implement the following code:

```
// function to reset password
    func resetPassword(emailAddress: String) {
        Auth.auth().sendPasswordReset(withEmail: emailAddress)
    }
```

This API from Firebase Auth will send a reset password email for us without implementing any backend code. We only need to pass the email from the frontend!

Let's now build the user interface for our screen. Head to `SignUpView` to make our reset password screen accessible.

Start with a State variable to handle the pop-up presentation:

```
@State private var showingSheet = false
```

We will then add a button at the top left of our screen and place the following modifier, right above the `.NavigationTile`:

```
.toolbar {
                ToolbarItemGroup(placement:
                .cancellationAction) {
```

```
Button {
    showingSheet.toggle()
} label: {
    Text("Forgot password?")
}
.sheet(isPresented: $showingSheet) {
    ResetPasswordView()
}
}
}
```

Great, now that we can access this screen, let's implement the functionality and the user interface. Let's add these few State variables first to the ResetPasswordView.swift file:

```
@State private var emailAddress: String = ""
@EnvironmentObject var authModel: AuthViewModel
@Environment(\.presentationMode) var presentationMode
```

These will be useful to connect our View Model, handling the email address we are passing and finally presenting our screen as a pop-up.

Now, let's implement a form to let the user provide their email:

```
NavigationStack {
        Form {
            Section {
                TextField("Email", text: $emailAddress)
                    .textContentType(.emailAddress)
                    .textInputAutocapitalization(.never)
                    .keyboardType(.emailAddress)
            }
            Section(footer: Text("Once sent, check your
            email to reset your password.")) {
```

```
            Button(
                action: {
                    authModel.
                    resetPassword(emailAddress:
                    emailAddress)
                }) {
                    Text("Send email link").bold()
                }
            }
        }.navigationTitle("Reset password")
            .toolbar {
                ToolbarItemGroup(placement:
                .confirmationAction) {
                    Button("Done") {
                        presentationMode.wrappedValue.
                        dismiss()
                    }
                }
            }
    }
```

As usual, we used a simple and native iOS API to build our user interface, so the user is familiar with it. We use the button to execute the function we implemented in the View Model and another button inside the toolbar to close the form.

Now, I invite you to go ahead, sign up with a real email, then log out, and check the reset password functionalities.

Enter your password and click "Send email link" and then go your mailbox (also your spam) as follows:

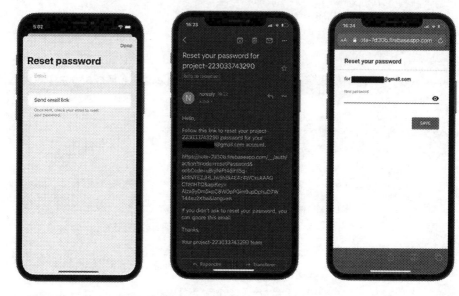

Figure 4-8. *Steps to follow to reset your password*

Once it is done, you can sign in again with your newly created password. Everything is handled by Firebase!

Secure the Firestore Database

Now that we have implemented a full user login flow, you might be wondering how to let the user access their own notes and not a collection accessible by everyone. That's what we are going to do in this section. For that we need to reorganize our database structure.

So far, it is composed of a collection called "Notes" that contains a series of documents that contain two string values: a text and an identifier.

This iteration will be slightly more complex and will look as follows:

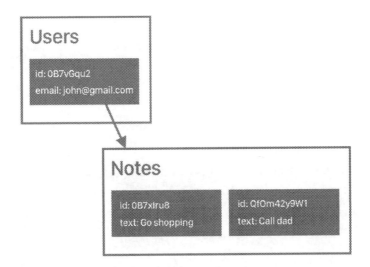

Figure 4-9. *Collection hierarchy of our iteration*

We will have a collection of users, and each user will have a subcollection of "Notes" containing a series of documents based on their input. It makes sense to operate with a subcollection since the user will be querying their own notes in our application.

It is time to register our user and create the collection. For this we need to save user information upon signup. We will do just that in the *AuthViewModel*, in the signup function.

First, let's import the Firestore framework at the top:

```
import FirebaseFirestore
```

Now, we will replace the current signup function with a more complete one that features the saving of user information to Firestore:

```
func signUp(emailAddress: String, password: String) {
    Auth.auth().createUser(withEmail: emailAddress,
    password: password) { result,  error in
        if let error = error {
```

```
            print("DEBUG: error \(error.
            localizedDescription)")
    } else {
            print("DEBUG: Succesfully created user with ID
            \(self.user?.uid ?? "")")
            guard let uid = Auth.auth().currentUser?.uid
            else { return }
Firestore.firestore().collection("Users").
document(uid).setData(["email" : emailAddress, "uid":
uid]) { err in
                if let err = err {
                    print(err)
                    return
                }
                print("Success")
            }

        }
    }
}
```

Great, now if there are no errors while signing up, we are saving our user information (email and identifier) under the collection "Users"; we are also debugging that in our console to check if the identifiers match.

Only one step is missing, editing the path of our database, so when you write a note, it is saved under your own user collection and not a top-level collection anymore.

But, first, let's clean up our Firestore database. Go ahead and delete the collection as follows:

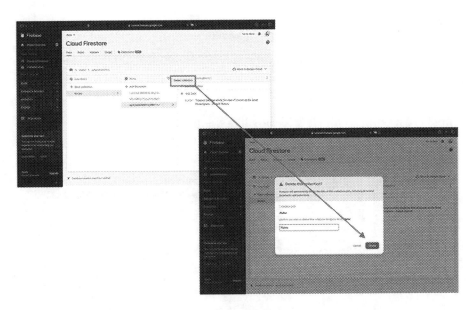

Figure 4-10. *Deleting a Firestore collection*

Now, we can change the current path

```
private var databaseReference = Firestore.firestore().
collection("Notes") // reference to our collection
```

to this one:

```
private lazy var databaseReference: CollectionReference? = {
        guard let user = Auth.auth().currentUser?.uid else
        {return nil}
    let ref = Firestore.firestore().collection("Users").
    document(user).collection("Posts")
    return ref
}()
```

We also need to import the Firebase Auth framework at the top of the NoteViewModel.swift file since we are checking the corresponding user identifier before moving forward:

91

import FirebaseAuth

Also, add a *?* after the database reference since we make it optional for safety.

You can now have fun and sign up a brand-new user and write a few notes. Then your database will look like the following path:

Users (collection) ➤ document ➤ ***Posts*** (collection) ➤ document

Figure 4-11. *Screenshots of the Firestore database matching our frontend data*

Security Rules

One last step is missing, securing our database from the Rules section.

So far, we are in development mode, which means everybody can read and write documents until 30 days after the creation of the database.

Since this Note application is private, we want to limit the ability to read and write data to authenticated users only, within their own user collection.

Go to the Firestore database ➤ Rules and type the followings rules in the console:

```
rules_version = '2';
service cloud.firestore {
```

```
match /databases/{database}/documents {
  match /Users/{uid}/{document=**} {
    allow read, write: if uid == request.auth.uid;
  }
 }
}
```

Then, click Publish:

Figure 4-12. *Editing rules in the Firestore database*

This code that we implemented will tell our database to restrict the access of our data to authenticated users only where their data match their identifier that was created when they signed up.

In practice, a user can only read, post, and edit their own notes. It is a crucial step before releasing any application to production as our previous rules would allow anyone on the Internet to access everyone's documents and user information.

Summary

With this chapter, we implemented a full authentication process with real-world business logic. Thanks to the Firebase SDK, we didn't even need to create our Model since FIRUser already provided us the necessary information.

We were able to post users' credentials to Firebase and match them against the response from the server, as well as implementing a password recovery with only one line of code!

Thanks to their listener APIs, we were also able to determine when a user session is active or terminated and present the appropriate screen.

With this being done, we have a fully working application, ready to be shipped on the App Store! It is now time to head to the next chapter with a brand-new application to build!

If you lost something on the way, find in the following a link to the repository of the application:

https://drive.google.com/drive/folders/1UWZ4 IDw5J81SxIjpjKd5QiSa5jR4mVHC?usp=share_link

Any source code or other supplementary material referenced by the author in this book is available to readers on the Github repository: https://github.com/Apress/Build-Mobile-Apps-with-SwiftUI-and-Firebase

CHAPTER 5

Advanced Firestore

Introducing Our New Project

Since we completed a note-taking application, we are now more comfortable with SwiftUI and the Firebase console. It is time to create a new application, this time with more complexity: there will be a feed view like that of famous social media platforms such as Instagram, a search feature, and a profile section where you can view your posts, and there is the ability to sign in seamlessly with your Apple account.

This chapter will focus on how to structure our database using Firestore, and I will introduce you to a larger model with more document types. By the end of it, you will be able to post and read a feed view and display a picture, a description, and a date when it is posted.

Here is what our application will look like:

© Sullivan De Carli 2023, corrected publication 2023
S. De Carli, *Build Mobile Apps with SwiftUI and Firebase*,
https://doi.org/10.1007/978-1-4842-9452-9_5

Figure 5-1. *Screenshots of our application*

Since there are many screens to be created, I prepared a starter file that you can download at the following link:

> *https://github.com/Apress/Build-Mobile-*
> *Apps-with-SwiftUI-and-firebase/tree/main/*
> *Socially%20chapter%205%20(starter)*

This file already has the following Swift packages installed:

- *FirebaseAuth*

- *FirebaseFirestore*

- *FirebaseFirestoreSwift*

- *FirebaseStorage*

Now, I invite you to start a new Firebase project. Click Add project and call it *Socially*:

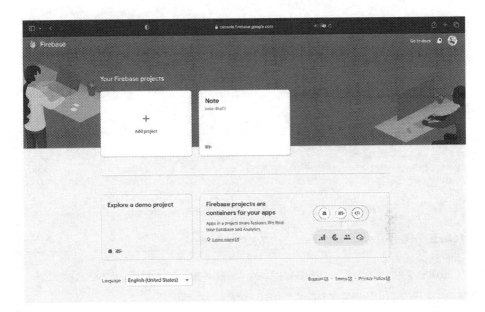

Figure 5-2. *Starting a new project in Firebase*

Why Are We Creating a New Firebase Project?

It is important to differentiate an application and a Firebase project. Overall, you should put in the same Firebase project applications that have a common business logic. Let's say you are building a competitor of User, the taxi ride application. As you want to reach a large market, you will be publishing on iOS and Android; therefore, you might be building four applications, two for the drivers and two for the riders on each platform. Since booking on Android or iOS is the same process on the backend, you can consider doing everything under the same Firebase project. Then, you will have something like this:

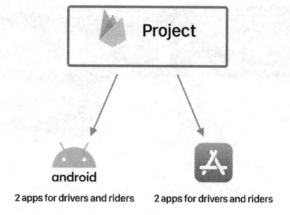

Figure 5-3. *Firebase project and applications*

Since, in our new project, we don't really share anything with the note-taking application, we are creating a new Firebase project.

Now, follow the step-by-step setup on the Firebase console and grab the *GoogleService-Info.plist* file and add it to the starter project. Once you have added the file and finished the five steps on the Firebase console, you can successfully run your project and connect to the Firebase backend.

Now that we have set up our project, let's code. As usual, we will start with our Model, create a new Swift file inside the *Model* folder, call it *Post*, and then copy/paste the following code:

```swift
import SwiftUI
import FirebaseFirestoreSwift

struct Post: Identifiable, Decodable {
    @DocumentID var id: String?
    var description: String?
    var imageURL: String?
    @ServerTimestamp var datePublished: Date?
}
```

So our Model that will be used for our Feed section is going to be composed of an identifier, a description, an image, and a date on which it has been published. The @*ServerTimestamp* comes from the Firebase APIs and gives us access to the server time. Then, the type Date is preferable to post a date.

Please, note that the image will be treated in our next chapter on Firebase Storage.

Let's dive into the View Model. Create a new file in the *View Model* folder and call it *PostViewModel* and then import these two frameworks at the top:

```
import SwiftUI
import FirebaseFirestore
```

We can create our class with our reference to the Model we created earlier and to our Firestore database:

```
class PostViewModel: ObservableObject {

    @Published var posts = [Post]()
    private var databaseReference = Firestore.firestore().
collection("Posts")

// Function to post data

}
```

And finally, here is our function to post data to the server:

```
// function to post data
    func addData(description: String, datePublished:
    Date) async {
        do {
            _ = try await databaseReference.addDocument(data:
            [ "description": description, "datePublished":
            datePublished])
```

```
    } catch {
        print(error.localizedDescription)
    }
}
```

This View Model is similar to what we have already done in Chapter 3, except that we are using the async/await method this time. You might be wondering what these keywords are for.

Call the Backend with Async/Await

In our application, we are uploading a few things – a picture and a description – and we are saving the date and time. The problem is the following: the data can take time to be uploaded to the server, especially if the picture is large.

Therefore, if we do a classic call, our user might be left on the screen for a few seconds while the picture is being uploaded to the database. This is not a great user experience. That's why we are using this method, so the call is asynchronous, and the user can safely navigate and await. While they are doing something else, the code is executed in the background.

Now that we have implemented our function to post, let's try it out! Head to the *PostView* file (already created in the starter project) and make a link with our View Model:

```
@ObservedObject private var viewModel = PostViewModel()
```

Then we simply call it inside the button where I left the comment:

```
// MARK: Post data to Firestore
Task {
  await self.viewModel.addData(description:   description,
  datePublished: Date())
      }
```

As you can see, we are saving the text input from the user. Regarding the date, we are passing *Date()*, which is taking the current iPhone date. For now, we don't do anything with the image since it is going to be the topic of our next chapter on Firebase Storage.

Additionally, we put the function inside a *Task*, which is necessary to be able to use the *await* key to inform our program that we must run this code in the background since it can take time to upload.

Now our frontend is ready to post data to the backend, but we still haven't set up Firestore to receive data. Head to the Firebase console, section Firestore Database, and click *Create database.* As with Chapter 3, enable the database in test mode:

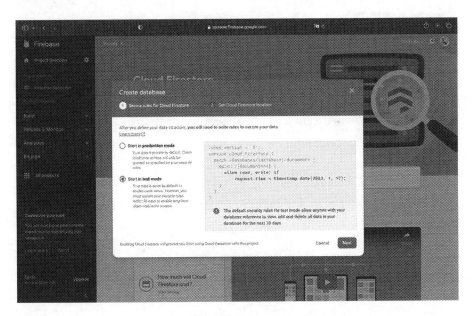

Figure 5-4. *Firestore – creating a database*

Then, we can run the application and try to post a comment. You should have it on your database:

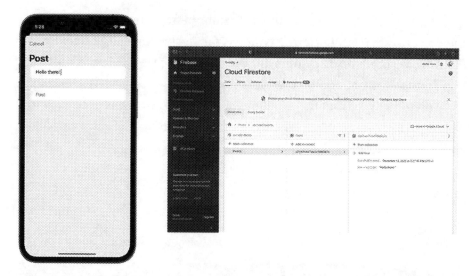

Figure 5-5. *Firebase Firestore console and application running*

Great, we have published data to Firestore with a text and the current date from our iPhone. It is now time to present this data that we just added.

For this, we will use a nice Firebase wrapper. First, add the following framework in the *FeedView*:

```
import FirebaseFirestoreSwift
```

Then, add the following code in the *FeedView*, right over the body variable:

```
@FirestoreQuery(collectionPath: "Posts")
var posts: [Post]
```

This way, we don't even need to implement a function inside our View Model. This is a great feature from Firebase APIs. It allows us to fetch data with only one line of code by just passing our Model together with the name we used for our Firebase collection.

Replace the current list in the FeedView with the following one:

```
List(posts) { posts in
              VStack(alignment: .leading) {
                  VStack {
                      Text(posts.description ?? "")
                          .font(.headline)
                          .padding(12)
                      Text("Published on the \(posts.
                      datePublished?.formatted() ?? "")")
                          .font(.caption)
                  }
              }.frame(minHeight: 100, maxHeight: 350)
    }
```

The *formatted()* modifier allows us to transform a data of type Date to String. This way, we can easily display a date in our application.

You can now run your application, and this will present the posts that you posted in a nice list.

Figure 5-6. *Figure of the list*

Summary

This chapter was pretty like Chapter 3 with a large model and an introduction to a new property wrapper from Firebase that made our life much easier.

We have seen how to handle not only data of type String but also Date. But we are not done with Firestore yet!

In this next chapter, we will still be using it to retrieve an image after we have uploaded it to our Storage. Let's discover how to handle large assets with Firebase.

You can have a look at the project at the following link, if you have lost something on the way:

> *https://github.com/Apress/Build-Mobile-Apps-with-SwiftUI-and-Firebase/tree/main/Socially%20chapter%205*

Any source code or other supplementary material referenced by the author in this book is available to readers on the Github repository: https://github.com/Apress/Build-Mobile-Apps-with-SwiftUI-and-Firebase

CHAPTER 6

Manage Pictures with Firebase Storage

We are looking to include pictures in our posts. The problem is the following: *Firestore* doesn't support such large documents. We can only add text, numbers, arrays, Booleans, timestamps, etc.

Therefore, Firebase introduced Storage. This is a package that lets us upload and download large data such as video, images, and audio documents. Through this chapter, we are going to see how to upload a picture to Firebase Storage, retrieve the URL where this picture is, and add it to the corresponding Firestore document.

Over this chapter, we will explore how to access the iPhone photo library, upload the picture to Storage, and retrieve it inside the Firestore backend. Let's get started!

Access the iPhone Camera and Library

Before uploading a picture, we first need to take one or, at least, let the user access the photo library from our application. In iOS 16, Apple introduced a new framework for SwiftUI: PhotosUI, which will let us select a picture with only a few lines of code.

Head to the *PostView* file, and import the framework:

```
import PhotosUI
```

© Sullivan De Carli 2023, corrected publication 2023
S. De Carli, *Build Mobile Apps with SwiftUI and Firebase*,
https://doi.org/10.1007/978-1-4842-9452-9_6

Once we have access to the framework, we can get access to *PhotosPickerItem*. Let's add the following two variables over the body variable:

```
@State var data: Data?
@State var selectedItem: [PhotosPickerItem] = []
```

The first variable is to observe the data we pass while selecting a picture. The second variable will let us observe what item the user is selecting (which picture).

It's now time to implement the user interface. Implement the following section inside the SwiftUI *Form of the PostView,* right over the two other sections already implemented:

```
Section {
                    PhotosPicker(selection: $selectedItem,
                    maxSelectionCount: 1, selectionBehavior:
                    .default, matching: .images,
                    preferredItemEncoding: .automatic) {
                        if let data = data, let image =
                        UIImage(data: data) {
                            Image(uiImage: image)
                                .resizable()
                                .scaledToFit()
                                .frame( maxHeight: 300)
                        } else {
                            Label("Select a picture",
                            systemImage: "photo.on.rectangle.
                            angled")
                        }
                    }.onChange(of: selectedItem) { newValue in
                        guard let item = selectedItem.
                        first else {
```

```
            return
        }
        item.loadTransferable(type: Data.self)
        { result in
            switch result {
            case .success(let data):
                if let data = data {
                    self.data = data
                }
            case .failure(let failure):
                print("Error: \(failure.
                localizedDescription)")
            }
        }
    }
}
```

Here, we are doing a few things. We are adding the *PhotosPicker* that lets us access the user library. We are passing a few things:

- selection – This is the item variable earlier.

- maxSelectionCount – We give the ability to only select one picture.

- matching – From there you can pass a series of things: only video, only images, just screenshots, etc. Here we will focus on images only.

- preferredItemEncoding – Here we left it to automatic, so the system will decide itself which resolution is better.

Then we created a label if there is no image selected; otherwise, we display the selected image.

That's it to access the photo library and display the image selected. The new APIs have made it easy for us to implement this feature. Prior to iOS 16, it was necessary to request authorization and implement some code and capabilities in Xcode. Here, Apple is handling everything, making it easier for us. You can try it out from the *PostView*.

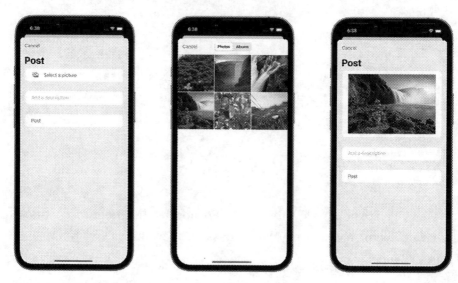

Figure 6-1. *Uploading a picture from the library*

Upload Pictures to Firebase Storage

Now that we have access to the pictures, it is time to upload this data in Firebase Storage. Let's head to the Firebase console and select Storage.

As usual, we need to do a bit of setup. Click *"Get started"* on the following screen:

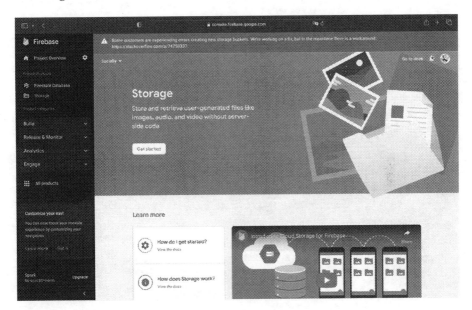

Figure 6-2. *"Get started" from Firebase Storage*

Next, you can select the test mode since we are going to secure the database at the end of our development phase:

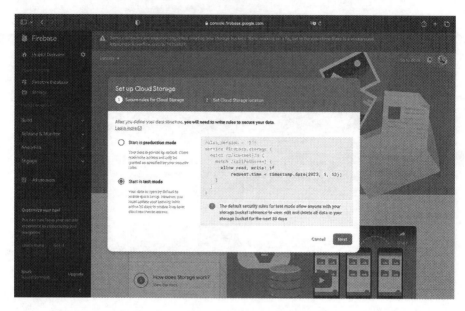

Figure 6-3. *Development mode*

Great, we are now ready to receive large assets from our application to the Firebase backend. Let's go back to code! Head to the *PostViewModel* file.

Import the Storage framework at the top of the file:

```
import FirebaseStorage
```

As usual, we need a reference to the database. Add the following line of code:

```
let storageReference = Storage.storage().reference().child
("\(UUID().uuidString)")
```

We need to implement this code to have a reference. We are using the storage APIs, and we are passing a Swift powerful feature: UUID. It basically creates a unique identifier every time it is called. This way, every time we upload an asset, we will have a different identifier for every single asset.

Now that we have a reference, we need to implement the function to upload an asset. Let's first add an additional parameter in the following function we created in the previous chapter:

```
func addData(description: String, datePublished: Date)
```

Replace the preceding function with the following:

```
func addData(description: String, datePublished: Date,
data: Data)
```

Great, now we can add the function to upload the data and download the URL where this image is stored.

Replace the current function *addData()* with the following:

```
func addData(description: String, datePublished: Date, data:
Data) async {
    do {
        _ = try await
        storageReference.putData(data, metadata: nil) {
        (metadata, error) in
            guard let metadata = metadata else {
                return
            }

            self.storageReference.downloadURL { (url,
            error) in
                guard let downloadURL = url else {
                    // Uh-oh, an error occurred!
                    return
```

```
                    }
                    self.databaseReference.addDocument(data:
                    [ "description": description,
                    "datePublished": datePublished, "imageURL":
                    downloadURL.absoluteString])

                }
            }
        } catch {
            print(error.localizedDescription)
        }
    }
```

Here we have added two important functions:

- putData – This basically takes the asset we have selected and upload it to the Firebase backend.

- downloadURL – This is responsible for grabbing the URL where the asset has been in the Firebase backend. This way, we are using this URL while passing the data to Firestore with *downloadURL.absoluteString*.

Integrate Large Documents with Firestore

Let's now call the function so we can upload documents to Firebase Storage in our View. Head to the *PostView* file.

You will see a warning telling you that you are missing a parameter named data. Let's correct that by replacing the call with the following one, which includes the data parameter:

```
await self.viewModel.addData(description: description,
datePublished: Date(), data: data!)
```

With the exclamation mark, we are saying in our program that we should have this data. Therefore, we need to prevent the user from clicking the button if there are no images selected. So add the following modifier after the button last graph:

```
.disabled(data == nil)
```

Great, now our function includes all that we need to upload a picture. You can go ahead and write another post, writing a description and selecting a picture. After this, check the Storage console. You should have the following:

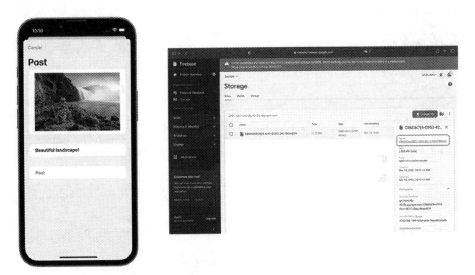

Figure 6-4. *Firebase Storage – new upload*

Our application has successfully uploaded an asset to the Firebase Storage backend. You can click the link on the right. It will open a new URL, downloading the picture we just uploaded. We basically put this data in a bucket, which generates a unique URL to store it.

Also, a unique identifier is generated from the frontend, thanks to the *UUID().uuidString* feature, that we use as a document reference.

Now, have a look at the Firebase Firestore document that you just uploaded:

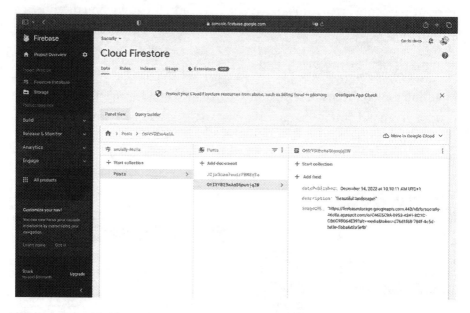

Figure 6-5. *Firebase Firestore – new document uploaded*

As you can see, we have a URL saved as a string under the field *imageURL*.

If you pay close attention, the URL is composed like this:

$https://firebasestorage.googleapis.com$ / [our project reference] / [the identifier we generated]

Once it is uploaded to Storage, this URL is downloaded with *storageReference.downloadURL* and added to our Firestore collection.

Fantastic! Now we can go ahead and read that image URL in our feed. To achieve that, we will use the SwiftUI *AsyncImage* modifier.

Add the following code in the *FeedView*, right over our two texts inside the *List*:

```
AsyncImage(url: URL(string: posts.imageURL ?? "")) {
phase in
                        switch phase {
                        case .empty:
                            EmptyView()
                        case .success(let image):
                          image                 .resizable()
                          .frame(width: 300, height: 200)
                            case .failure:
                    Image(systemName: "photo")
                        @unknown default:
                            EmptyView()

                        }
            }
```

This code is useful to get an image from a URL. *AsyncImage* already handles the asynchronous call. We also pass an *EmptyView* in case the server is returning no image.

We now have our feed screen created matching the documents we have in Firestore:

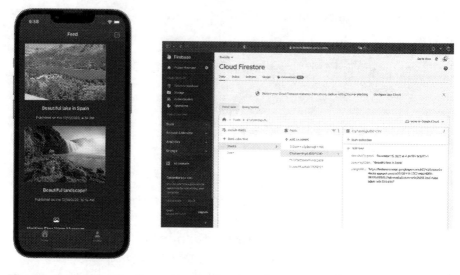

Figure 6-6. *Our feed screen displaying documents from Firestore*

Summary

Through this chapter, we have implemented a SwiftUI photo picker with only a few lines of code. We then extracted the data picked by the user and stored it. Following this, we introduced Firebase Storage and stored the file in a bucket with a unique link. Then, we downloaded the URL where the data was stored to add it to our Firestore document.

Thanks to this process, we can enrich our application with assets. We could even have used video like successful social media sites such as *TikTok* and *Instagram*.

Please, find at the following link the source code of this chapter:

https://drive.google.com/drive/folders/19cPy xU8AYdW_8ObUZOhxryLBLPx8qtRQ?usp=share_link

It is now time to head to our next chapter: implementing the login flow. This time, we will use "Sign in with Apple."

Any source code or other supplementary material referenced by the author in this book is available to readers on the Github repository: https:// github.com/Apress/Build-Mobile-Apps-with-SwiftUI-and-Firebase

CHAPTER 7

Authenticate with Apple

Over this chapter, we will go back to Firebase Auth, but this time we are going to implement a better user experience. Instead of requiring email and password, we will be presenting "Sign in with Apple."

Additionally, we will let the user access our application even if they don't have an account, and we will restrict the ability to post to registered users only with Firestore rules, in the next chapter.

This logic will look like the following:

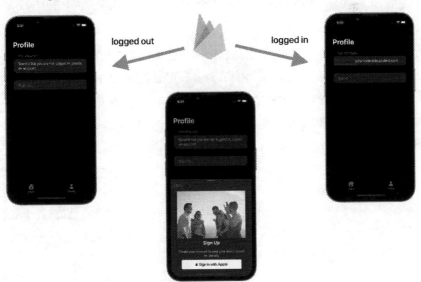

Figure 7-1. *Logic of the signup flow*

© Sullivan De Carli 2023, corrected publication 2023
S. De Carli, *Build Mobile Apps with SwiftUI and Firebase*,
https://doi.org/10.1007/978-1-4842-9452-9_7

Set Up the Project and "Sign in with Apple"

Sign in with Apple has been introduced with iOS 13 and allows the user to use their Apple ID (the one they generally use for iCloud or App Store purchases) for signing up to your application. It is highly recommended to add it since it's more user-friendly, there's no need to remember a password, you sign up in one click, and the user can hide the email with Apple private relay. As always, it is a great privacy enhancement provided by Apple.

How does it work with Firebase?

Firebase provides an API to work with Apple sign-in, to sign up a user. It will make the call to the Apple server to verify the identity, furnish a callback response to Firebase that will register our user in the database, and send back to us a response stating that the signup has been successful or unsuccessful if it has returned any errors.

As with email and password, we still have access to the User object provided by Firebase. So we can go ahead and implement the function in the View Model and then the native Apple button in the user interface.

Important note   To work with Sign in with Apple, you need an Apple developer account, which costs $99 a year. If you don't want to sign up for a developer account, you can still follow this chapter. You simply need to use the signup and sign-in code with the email and password that I left as commented in the starter file.

First, we need to add the capabilities to use Sign in with Apple. Head to the main target. Under Signing & Capabilities, search for "*Sign in with Apple*" and then press Enter as follows:

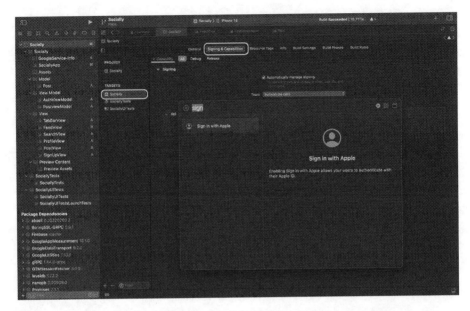

Figure 7-2. *Xcode* ➤ *Signing & Capabilities – Sign in with Apple*

If it doesn't appear on the search, you might have your membership or a certificate expired. Check your Apple developer account.

Now that we have set up Sign in with Apple in Xcode, it is time to add it on the Firebase console. Head to your console and click "Get started." For the sign-in method, select Apple, enable, and save.

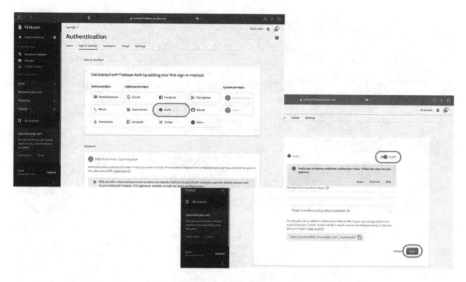

Figure 7-3. *Firebase console – enabling Sign in with Apple*

We have now completed all the setup to work with Sign in with Apple. Now it is time to code. Let's head to our View Model to implement the necessary functions to work with Sign in with Apple.

Integrate "Sign in with Apple"

It's now time to code. The first thing to do is to head to *AuthViewModel* and import the necessary framework to work with Apple authentication:

```
import AuthenticationServices
import CryptoKit
```

The framework *AuthenticationServices* is necessary to talk with the Apple server, and CryptoKit lets us create a cryptography key that allows us to pass the data in a secure way.

Now, go to the *AuthViewModel* file, and add these two variables:

```
@Published var user: User?
var currentNonce: String?
```

We are using the User object from the Firebase Auth framework again and a *String* that we will use to generate a unique key to pass our data.

Now, you can implement the following two functions:

```
func randomNonceString(length: Int = 32) -> String {
    precondition(length > 0)
    let charset: [Character] =
    Array("0123456789ABCDEFGHIJKLMNOPQRSTUVXYZabcdefghijklm
    nopqrstuvwxyz-._")
    var result = ""
    var remainingLength = length

    while remainingLength > 0 {
      let randoms: [UInt8] = (0 ..< 16).map { _ in
        var random: UInt8 = 0
        let errorCode = SecRandomCopyBytes(kSecRandomDefault,
        1, &random)
        if errorCode != errSecSuccess {
          fatalError(
            "Unable to generate nonce. SecRandomCopyBytes
            failed with OSStatus \(errorCode)"
          )
        }
        return random
      }

      randoms.forEach { random in
        if remainingLength == 0 {
          return
        }
```

```
    if random < charset.count {
      result.append(charset[Int(random)])
      remainingLength -= 1
    }
  }
}

  return result
}
```

Great! We have now completed all this first piece. This piece of code is suggested by the Firebase documentation. It is useful to create a node for passing the data from the frontend to the Apple server. Also add the following function:

```
func sha256(_ input: String) -> String {
    let inputData = Data(input.utf8)
    let hashedData = SHA256.hash(data: inputData)
    let hashString = hashedData.compactMap {
      String(format: "%02x", $0)
    }.joined()
    return hashString
}
```

This one is to implement the SHA-256 protocol, a world-class cryptography protocol used also in the Bitcoin blockchain, for example. Now that we have added the function, we can go ahead to the View: *SignUpView*.

At the top of the file, import the following framework to access the Apple sign-in button and Firebase authentication:

```
import AuthenticationServices
import FirebaseAuth
import FirebaseFirestore
```

Then, observe our View Model by adding this code over the *body* variable:

```
@ObservedObject private var authModel = AuthViewModel()
```

We can now implement the following code in the *SignUpView*, inside the *VStack*:

```
SignInWithAppleButton(onRequest:  { request in
        let nonce = authModel.randomNonceString()
        authModel.currentNonce = nonce
        request.requestedScopes = [.email]
        request.nonce = authModel.sha256(nonce)
    },
        onCompletion: { result in
        //Completion
        switch result {
        case .success(let authResults):
            switch authResults.credential {
            case let appleIDCredential as
            ASAuthorizationAppleIDCredential:
                guard let nonce = authModel.
                currentNonce else {
                    fatalError("Invalid state: A login
                    callback was received, but no login
                    request was sent.")
                }
                guard let appleIDToken = appleIDCredential.
                identityToken else {
                    fatalError("Invalid state: A login
                    callback was received, but no login
                    request was sent.")
                }
```

```
        guard let idTokenString = String(data: appleIDToken,
        encoding: .utf8) else {
                print("Unable to serialize token
                string from data: \(appleIDToken.
                debugDescription)")
                return
        }
        let credential = OAuthProvider.credential
        (withProviderID: "apple.com",idToken:
        idTokenString,rawNonce: nonce)
        Auth.auth().signIn(with: credential) {
        (authResult, error) in
            if (error != nil) {
                print(error?.localized
                Description as Any)
                return
            }
            print("signed in")
            guard let user = authResult?.user else
            { return }

      let userData = [
"email": user.email, "uid": user.uid ]
                Firestore.firestore().
                collection("User")
                    .document(user.uid)
                    .setData(userData) { _ in
print("DEBUG: Did upload user data.")
                    }
                }
print("\(String(describing: Auth.auth().currentUser?.uid))")
```

```
            default:
                break
            }
        default:
            break
        }
    }
).signInWithAppleButtonStyle(.black)
.frame(width: 290, height: 45, alignment: .center)
```

We just implemented the native Sign in with Apple button in which we are passing the credentials handled by the user through the Apple service. We are also checking if the credentials are being passed correctly with the *guard let* statements.

Since we are going to present this *SignUpView* from the *ProfileView*, we need to handle the presentation from there. We need to incorporate a logic to show the signup screen when there is no user and display user info when they have signed up. For this, we need to head to *AuthViewModel* and integrate these two functions:

```
func listenToAuthState() {
    Auth.auth().addStateDidChangeListener { [weak self] _,
    user in
        guard let self = self else {
            return
        }
        self.user = user
    }
}
```

This will help us listen for changes from the Firebase Auth framework. We also need to implement the logout function:

```
func signOut() {
        do {
            try Auth.auth().signOut()
        } catch let signOutError as NSError {
            print("Error signing out: %@", signOutError)
        }
    }
```

Great! Now we can build the user interface in the *ProfileView*. Let's observe this Boolean for handling the presentation and our *ViewModel* of the *SignUpView*:

```
@State private var showSignUp: Bool = false
@ObservedObject private var authModel = AuthViewModel()
```

And add the following code inside the *body* variable:

```
VStack(alignment: .center) {
            if authModel.user != nil {
                Form {
                    Section("you account") {
                        Text(authModel.user?.email ?? "")
                    }
                    Button {
                        authModel.signOut()
                    } label: {
                        Text("logout")
                            .foregroundColor(.red)
                    }
                }
```

```
    } else {
        Form {
            Section("you account") {
                Text("Seem's like you are not logged
                in, create an account")
            }
            Button {
                showSignUp.toggle()
            } label: {
                Text("Sign Up")
                    .foregroundColor(.blue)
                    .bold()
            }.sheet(isPresented: $showSignUp) {
                SignUpView().presentationDetents([.
                medium, .large])
            }
        }
    }
}.onAppear { authModel.listenToAuthState() }
```

Now our UI is ready, presenting the email of the user when logged in or a button where there is no session detected by the Firebase server. We are going to pass all that we need to the Apple server.

What can we expect from the response?

- A unique relay email or their original email

- Their full name (optional – we are not asking for it for this project)

Following that, on completion, we will be able to proceed and register the credentials onto Firebase. Now, we could check our Firebase console to see if we had correctly signed up our user. *(I recommend checking this feature on a real device.)*

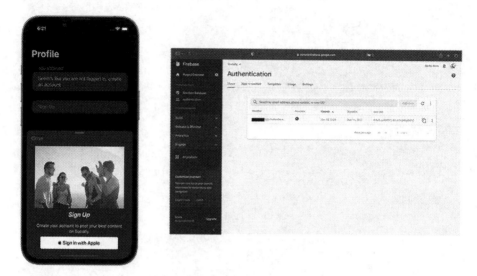

Figure 7-4. *Sign in with Apple working with Firebase Auth*

Summary

We explored the Firebase authenticate SDK with a more advanced feature: Sign in with Apple. Thanks to their APIs, we were able to authenticate the user. However, Sign in with Apple requires a bit more setup since we need to talk to both the Apple server and Firebase server to get a response.

Thanks to their great listener, we were also able to determine whether our user is signed in or not, and from this response, we presented the right screen.

Now that we know how to use Sign in with Apple, I have a challenge for you: integrate Sign in with Apple with our Note application that we created over Chapters 3 and 4.

If you missed something while following this chapter, you can check this source code:

Any source code or other supplementary material referenced by the author in this book is available to readers on the Github repository: https://github.com/Apress/Build-Mobile-Apps-with-SwiftUI-and-Firebase

CHAPTER 8

Adding Features Without Coding

We have created a nice basis for a social media application, but it is not completed yet. There are many areas of improvements and a few features to be implemented.

Over this chapter, we will be working on *Socially* by implementing a feature to resize the images uploaded on the backend, so they are downsized and can be presented faster to our end user. We will achieve this thanks to Firebase Extension: a great no-code tool to implement functionalities on the backend without writing code.

Finally, we will secure our database, so certain data is only accessible to the current user. We will also restrict the ability to post content to registered users only.

Exploring Firebase Extension

Firebase Extension is a framework developed by Firebase to allow you to implement functionalities on the backend without writing any code. Some have been developed by Firebase such as triggering images, sending data to Google BigQuery, or resizing an image. It also includes many third-party providers like Stripe for running subscriptions and Algolia to search inside Firestore documents, integrates in-app purchase with RevenueCat, and many more.

© Sullivan De Carli 2023, corrected publication 2023
S. De Carli, *Build Mobile Apps with SwiftUI and Firebase*,
https://doi.org/10.1007/978-1-4842-9452-9_8

We will get started with Resize Images made by Firebase.

This functionality will be useful in our application since the users are uploading images to the database and retrieving them in our feed. This functionality will resize the images to a determined size and therefore reduce the size. This will make our application much more efficient!

To install this extension, you need to upgrade your Firebase project to the Blaze plan. This means Google will be able to charge you for using the function you are implementing on the backend. It is only going to represent a few cents for the tests we are going to execute.

Head to the Firebase console ➤ Build ➤ Extensions. Then look for *Resize Images* and click Install.

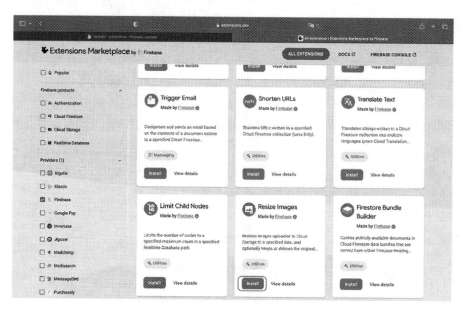

Figure 8-1. *Firebase Extension marketplace*

If you haven't subscribed to the Blaze plan yet, the console will invite you to upgrade. Follow the steps and enter your credit card information. If you correctly followed the instructions, you would have the following pop-up:

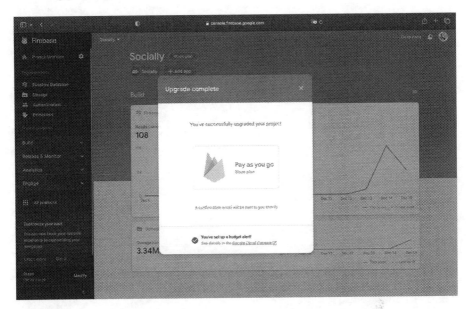

Figure 8-2. *Project updated to the Blaze plan*

Now, you can start installing the extension. Follow the four steps provided by Firebase, and you can edit the followings fields:

– Backfill existing images – No

– Sizes of resized images: 320 × 200

This way, Firebase will automatically resize the images to 320×200 pixels, so it looks nice on our screen and the overall weight of the file will be reduced. You can click Install extension; it will take a few minutes to take effect:

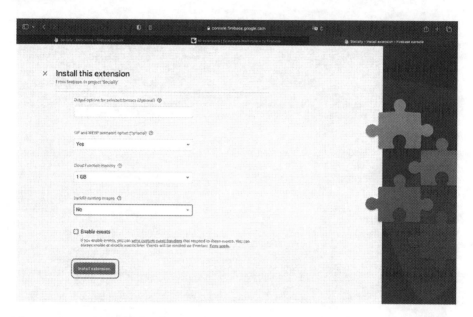

Figure 8-3. *Installing the Firebase extension*

You can now test your application by publishing a post with an image. The images will be retrieved faster since they have been downsized by the backend. Therefore, we have improved our application in a few minutes without writing any code.

Track Our App Usage with Analytics

It is useful to figure out how our users are using our application, to determine our conversion for signup, for example (how many users create an account / how many users download the app). Thanks to Firebase, it is easy to implement this tracker with Google Analytics.

The first thing to do is add the Firebase Analytics package to our application. Head to your main target. Under *General* scroll down to *Frameworks, Libraries, and Embedded Content* and click the plus button. Then select *FirebaseAnalytics* and click *Add.*

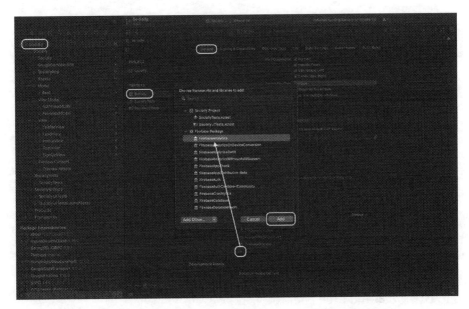

Figure 8-4. *Adding a package to the project*

Now we are ready to use the Firebase analytics APIs. First thing I want to check is how many users are converting to authenticated users. To do so, I need to add an event every time a user successfully signs up.

Let's head to *SignUpView* and import the framework at the top:

```
import FirebaseAnalytics
```

Then, add the following line of code right after the *print(signed in)* – this way, we are sure the authentication has been successful:

```
Analytics.logEvent("user_sign_up",
parameters: nil)
```

That's it. In one line of code, we have logged an event to Firebase to see each user that signed up to our application.

You can check in the Firebase console ➤ Analytics ➤ Events in the next 24 hours. You will see the events logged each time a user authenticates.

Securing Our Database

One final step is left before releasing our application to the public: secure our database. Since we are using Firestore, we need to head to this part in the console and edit the rules.

Right now, everybody can write posts and read user information on our database without being authenticated. It is a concern for security and cost.

Therefore, we need to restrict the ability to write data for authenticated users only, but we can allow anyone to read since profiles are public, as well as posts in our application.

Head to the Firebase console ➤ Firestore ➤ Rules and implement the following rules and then click Publish:

```
rules_version = '2';
service cloud.firestore {
  match /databases/{database}/documents {
    match /{document=**} {
      allow read: if true;
      allow write: if request.auth != null;
    }
  }
}
```

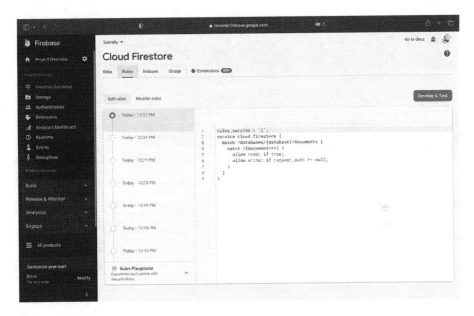

Figure 8-5. *Cloud Firestore rules*

Now nobody can write anything if they didn't sign up. We have usefully restricted the access of our data!

Summary

Over this last chapter, we explored Firebase Extension, the no-code tool to enhance our application with additional features. Then we logged events to see how our users are using our application, here with each time someone authenticates on our application.

Finally, we secured our database to disable anyone who doesn't sign up to post any document on Firestore.

That closes our book. Thank you for following along! You can find the source code of the final project at the following link:

https://drive.google.com/drive/folders/1eF-OXxC1jnOOb3OBsfXOFH7LzV2w24pU?usp=share_link

Any source code or other supplementary material referenced by the author in this book is available to readers on the Github repository: https://github.com/Apress/Build-Mobile-Apps-with-SwiftUI-and-Firebase

Correction to: Build Mobile Apps with SwiftUI and Firebase

Correction to:

Sullivan De Carli, *Build Mobile Apps with SwiftUI and Firebase*
https://doi.org/10.1007/978-1-4842-9452-9

This book has been published without the below corrections incorporated and all of which has been incorporated.

1. At the end of each chapter, the below github link has been added `https://github.com/Apress/Build-Mobile-Apps-with-SwiftUI-and-Firebase`

2. The author name in the cover reads "Carli" which has been updated as "De Carli"

The updated version of this book can be found at
https://doi.org/10.1007/978-1-4842-9452-9

© Sullivan De Carli 2023
S. De Carli, *Build Mobile Apps with SwiftUI and Firebase*,
https://doi.org/10.1007/978-1-4842-9452-9_9

3. In chapter 5, the following link has been replaced on page 96 of the printed version (instead of the Google drive link): `https://github.com/Apress/Build-Mobile-Apps-with-SwiftUI-and-firebase/tree/main/Socially%20chapter%205%20(starter)`

5. In chapter 5, in page 104, the below link has been updated in the summary instead of the Google drive link: `https://github.com/Apress/Build-Mobile-Apps-with-SwiftUI-and-Firebase/tree/main/Socially%20chapter%205`

Index

A

addData() function, 111
addDocument APIs, 50
Algolia, 129
Apple authentication, 120
Apple ID, 118
Apple server, 118, 120, 122, 127, 128
Arrays, 105
AsyncImage, 115
AuthenticationServices
      framework, 120
AuthViewModel, 75, 80, 85, 89, 120

B

Backend as a service (BaaS), 17
Bitcoin blockchain, 122
Blaze plan, 130, 131
Booleans, 63, 105, 126

C

ContentView.swift file, 50, 52, 55,
      56, 66, 84
Create-Read-Update-Delete
      (CRUD), 43, 71
CryptoKit, 120

D

Data parameter, 112
downloadURL.absoluteString
      function, 112
downloadURL function, 112

E

Embedded Content, 133
EmptyView, 115

F

Feed screen, 116
FeedView, 102, 103, 115
Firebase
    add iOS app, 30
    advantages, 19
    Apple app, 32, 33, 36, 39, 41
    BaaS, 17
    cloud service, iOS
      application, 17, 18
    connect iOS application
      GoogleService-Info.
      plist, 34, 35
    SDK, 35
    Xcode (*see* Xcode)

Firebase (*cont.*)
    dashboard, 25, 26
    disadvantages, 20
    Firestore section, 47
    Google Analytics, 22, 23
    Homepage, 21
    iOS application, 18, 19
    project name, 22
    select Google Analytics
        account, 24
    Spark plan label, 26
Firebase Analytics package, 133, 134
Firebase authentication, 122
Firebase Auth framework, 91,
    121, 126
Firebase Auth SDK
    authentication section, 73
    email/password selection, 74
    enable provider and save, 74
    logic implementation, 77
    manage user sessions, 75–79
    secure firestore database
        collection hierarchy, 89
        delete Firestore collection, 91
        import, 91
        security rules, 92, 93
        signup function, 89
    sign up with email and
        password
        app run/post user data, 83
        AuthViewModel, 80, 84
        reset password, 85, 87, 88
        sign-in process, 83
        SignUpView, 81

    user interface, 81
    View Model, 82, 84
    Xcode, 79
Firebase collection, 102
Firebase console, 15, 17, 21, 24, 25,
    27, 29, 30, 35, 46, 47, 69, 73,
    83, 95, 98, 101, 108, 119,
    120, 127
Firebase documentation,
    17, 27, 122
Firebase extension
    exploration, 129–132
    installation, 132
    marketplace, 130
    no-code tool, 129, 135
Firebase Firestore, 43, 114
Firebase Firestore console, 54, 102
Firebase project
    Async/Await, backend, 100–103
    creation, 97–99
Firebase server, 127, 128
Firebase Software Development
    Kit (SDK), 35
Firebase Storage, 37, 99, 101, 105–116
Firestore
    create database, 46–55
    database, 92
    delete data, 65–68
    document, 105
    MVVM design pattern, 44–46
    NoSQL document-based
        database, 43
    note application, 43
    pass data, views, 58–62

read data, 55–58

two-step setup, 48

upload data, 55

FIRUser, 76, 94

formatted() modifier, 103

Frameworks, 133

G, H

Google Analytics, 19, 20, 22–24, 132

Google BigQuery, 129

GoogleService-Info.plist, 34, 69, 98

I, J, K

imageURL field, 114

import FirebaseAnalytics, 133

import FirebaseStorage, 110

import PhotosUI, 105

Integrating documents, 112–115

iOS 16, 108

iPhone, 102

iPhone camera and library access, 105, 107, 108

iPhone photo library, 105

L

Libraries, 133

listenToAuthState(), 76

M

Matching, 107

maxSelectionCount, 107

MVVM design pattern, 44–46, 69

N, O

NavigationLink, 59, 60, 62

NavigationView, 55, 60

NoteViewModel, 49, 65

Numbers, 105

P, Q

PhotosPicker, 106, 107

PhotosUI, 105

Picture uploading, firebase storage, 108, 110–112

PostView file, 100, 105, 112

PostViewModel, 99, 110

preferredItemEncoding, 107

ProfileView function, 125, 126

putData() function, 112

R

RevenueCat, 129

S

Securing database, 134, 135

@ServerTimestamp, 99

SF Symbols, 53

SHA-256 protocol, 122

Sign in with Apple, 117

advanced feature, 128

integration, 120–123, 125–127

note application, 128

project set up, 118, 119

view model, 120

in Xcode, 119

SignUpView function, 122, 125, 126

Social media, 95, 116, 129

Storage console, 113

storageReference.downloadURL, 114

String, 104

Swift language, 4

Swift packages, 35, 41, 96

SwiftUI, 44, 57, 67

    in 2019, Apple, 8

    AsyncImage modifier, 114

    code, 10

    identifiable, 13

    map application, 14, 15

    MapKit, 12

    photo picker, 116

    UIKit, 8–10

    Xcode, 1–8

T

Taxi ride application, 97

Text, 105

Timestamps, 105

U

UIKit, 8–10

UITableViewDataSource, 10

User interface, 1, 6–8, 10, 11, 13, 20,
    44, 46, 50, 53, 60–62, 65, 69,
    79, 81, 82, 84–87, 106,
    118, 126

UUID, 111, 113

V, W

viewDidLoad method, 10

View model, 44, 46, 49, 50,
    54, 56, 77, 78, 86, 99,
    100, 102, 123

X, Y, Z

Xcode

    add package, 37, 38

    Apple, 1

    App Store, 2

    drag and drop the
        GoogleService-Info.plist
        file, 34

    identifier, 31

    Mac App Store, 1

    new project, 29

    NoteApp.swift, 39

    run and communication to
        Firebase, 40

    select App template, 27, 28

    settings, project, 5

    Simulator app, 8

    simulator run, 7, 12

    Swift language, 4

    tabs, 6

    template, 4

    14.1 version, 2

    welcome screen, 3, 27

Printed in the United States
by Baker & Taylor Publisher Services